THE ARMS OF TIME

Sibbie by Augustus John

RUPERT HART-DAVIS

The Arms of Time

A MEMOIR

In the dark twilight of an autumn morn,
I stood within a little country-town,
Wherefrom a long acquainted path went down
To the dear village haunts where I was born;
The low of oxen on the rainy wind,
Death and the Past, came up the well-known road,
And bathed my heart with tears, but stirr'd my mind
To tread once more the track so long untrod;
But I was warn'd, 'Regrets which are not thrust
Upon thee, seek not; for this sobbing breeze
Will but unman thee; thou art bold to trust
Thy woe-worn thoughts among these roaring trees,
And gleams of by-gone playgrounds – Is't no crime
To rush by night into the arms of Time?'

CHARLES TENNYSON TURNER

HAMISH HAMILTON
LONDON

First published in Great Britain 1979
by Hamish Hamilton Ltd
Garden House 57–59 Long Acre London WC2E 9JZ

Copyright © 1979 by Rupert Hart-Davis

British Library Cataloguing in Publication Data

Hart-Davis, Sir Rupert
   The arms of time.
   1. Hart-Davis, Sybil Mary
   2. England – Biography
   I. Title
   942.082′092′4   CT788.H/
   ISBN 0-241-10305-3

Printed and bound in Great Britain at
The Camelot Press Ltd, Southampton

To my beautiful sister
DEIRDRE
with a lifetime's
admiration, gratitude
and love

CONTENTS

ILLUSTRATIONS

PROLOGUE : THE FEMALE LINE

Pardon, old fathers, if you still remain
Somewhere in ear-shot for the story's end.

W. B. YEATS

[1]

'IT'S THE Mrs Jordan blood coming out!' So said my Aunt Marie whenever any of her family behaved in a way that seemed to her outrageous, or even mildly unconventional. She had ample occasion to use the phrase, but I sometimes wondered whether the offending fluid that ran in our veins, however much diluted by several generations of Scottish noblemen, might not be to our advantage; for Mrs Jordan had many admirable qualities.

Certainly her early life was a trifle irregular, but she had much to contend with. Originally Dorothy Bland, she was born in London in 1761, of parents so insecurely married that when she was thirteen her Irish father, without benefit of divorce, abandoned her actress mother and their four children to marry an heiress. Dorothy made her first stage appearance in Dublin, but after three years she was seduced by an impresario called Richard Daly and fled pregnant to England, accompanied by her mother. There she was rescued by Tate Wilkinson, who ran the Yorkshire circuit of theatres. He recorded that at their first meeting he asked Dorothy whether she thought her talents were best suited to Tragedy, genteel or low Comedy, or Opera. She answered '*To all*'. Wilkinson was so amused by this self-confidence that he engaged her. She opened at Leeds in July 1782 as Calista in *The Fair Penitent* by Nicholas Rowe, and toured with Wilkinson for three years, with a brief interval for the birth of Daly's daughter. According to Wilkinson it was at his suggestion that she adopted the name Jordan because she had crossed the water from Ireland.

In 1785 she moved to London and made her début at Drury Lane as

Peggy in *The Country Girl*, Garrick's adaptation of Wycherley's play, and shortly afterwards set up house with a feckless barrister called Richard Ford. She bore him three children, two of whom survived, but despite renewed promises he never married her.

Her success at Drury Lane was rapid and enduring. Many of the plays are now forgotten, but some are not. Of Shakespeare's heroines she played Viola, Imogen, Rosalind, Ophelia, Juliet, Miranda and Beatrice. For Sheridan she created the rôle of Cora in *Pizarro*, and in revivals played Lydia Languish in *The Rivals*, Lady Teazle in *The School for Scandal*, and (most successfully) Miss Hoyden in *A Trip to Scarborough* (Byron described her performance as 'superlative'). Other successes included Kate Hardcastle in Goldsmith's *She Stoops to Conquer*, Miss Prue in Congreve's *Love for Love*, Corinna in Vanbrugh's *The Confederacy*, Fidelia in Wycherley's *The Plain Dealer*, and leading parts in three plays by Farquhar: Sir Harry Wildair in *The Constant Couple*, Sylvia in *The Recruiting Officer*, and Miss Sullen in *The Beaux Stratagem*. A goodly repertoire.

It is usually impossible to recapture the quality of long-dead actors, but Mrs Jordan had great allies. She was painted by Romney, Hoppner, Morland, Stothard and others. Coleridge told Byron that a Miss Hudson 'pronounced the blank verse of Shakespeare, and indeed verse in general, better than I ever heard it pronounced, with the solitary exception of some passages by Mrs Jordan'. Leigh Hunt wrote of her:

> There was one comic actress who was nature herself in one of her most genial forms. This was Mrs Jordan; who, though she was neither beautiful, nor handsome, nor even pretty, nor accomplished, nor 'a lady', nor anything conventional or *comme il faut* whatsoever, yet was so pleasant, so cordial, so natural, so full of spirits, so healthily constituted in mind and body, had such a shapely leg withal, so charming a voice, and such a happy and happy-making expression of countenance, that she appeared something superior to all those requirements of acceptability, and to hold a patent from nature herself for our delight and good opinion . . . she made even Methodists love her.

Sir Joshua Reynolds was 'quite enchanted with the being who ran upon the stage as a playground and laughed from sincere wildness of delight'. Charles Lamb said that in her heyday her voice 'sank, with her steady melting eye, into the heart'; and William Hazlitt was even more enthusiastic:

Mrs Jordan's excellences were all natural to her. It was not as an actress, but as herself, that she charmed every one. Nature had formed her in her most prodigal humour; and when nature is in the humour to make a woman all that is delightful, she does it most effectually. Mrs Jordan was the same in all her characters, and inimitable in all of them, because there was no one else like her. Her face, her tones, her manner, were irresistible. Her smile had the effect of sunshine, and her laugh did one good to hear it. Her voice was eloquence itself: it seemed as if her heart was always at her mouth. She was all gaiety, openness, and good-nature. She rioted in her fine animal spirits, and gave more pleasure than any other actress because she had the greatest spirit of enjoyment in herself.

And lastly Hazlitt again:

Mrs Jordan, the child of nature, whose voice was a cordial to the heart, because it came from it, rich, full, like the luscious juice of the ripe grape; to hear whose laugh was to drink nectar . . . Her person was large, soft, and generous like her soul . . . Mrs Jordan had nothing dexterous or knowing about her. She was Cleopatra turned into an oyster-wench, without knowing that she was Cleopatra, or caring that she was an oyster-wench. An oyster-wench, such as she was, would have been equal to a Cleopatra; and an Antony would not have deserted her for the empire of the world.

Most of these words might have been used to describe that latter-day enchantress Ellen Terry. I have quoted them at length because they seem to me to tell us exactly what Mrs Jordan was like on the stage, and because many of her qualities were inherited by her descendants. There is no doubt that if Mrs Siddons was the Tragic Muse of the day, Mrs Jordan was her counterpart in Comedy. The only time they played the same part – Rosalind in *As You Like It* – Mrs Siddons's biographer Thomas Campbell was forced to admit that 'here alone, I believe, in her whole professional career, Mrs Siddons found a rival who beat her out of a single character . . . Mrs Jordan was perhaps a little too much of the romp in some touches of the part; but altogether she had the *naïveté* of it to a degree that Shakespeare himself, if he had been a living spectator, would have gone behind the scenes to have saluted her for her success in it'.

*Mrs Jordan as Viola by
John Hoppner*

[2]

Towards the end of 1790 Prince William, Duke of Clarence, the third son of King George III, fell deeply in love with this radiant creature. She, after one more vain attempt to coax Richard Ford into matrimony, agreed to set up house with her royal lover, first at Clarence Lodge, Petersham, and then at Bushy Park, near Hampton Court. William had been trained as a sailor, but was now unemployed. He was incorrigibly uxorious, always in debt, bluff and outspoken in speech, occasionally some said a trifle dotty. But he was a good man, a faithful husband, and later an unexpectedly successful monarch. His twenty years with Mrs Jordan were domestically calm, happy – and fruitful, for between 1794 and 1807 ten children were born to this strangely diverse pair. They were surnamed Fitzclarence, and popularly known as The Great Illegitimates.

Both parents were devoted to them. And all the time, with ten brief intervals, Mrs Jordan continued on her brilliant theatrical way. Whenever she was acting out of London she wrote to the Duke every day, sometimes twice a day, and often included money from her theatrical earnings. Her letters are artless and misspelt but full of affection for the Duke and their children. In 1797 Clarence described her to a friend as 'one of the most perfect women in this world'.

She was certainly a devoted mother, a faithful consort, and a hard-working actress of brilliance. Nor was she without wit. When the Duke, at the King's instigation, wrote her a note suggesting that he should halve her allowance, she sent him back the bottom part of a playbill, reading 'No money returned after the rising of the curtain'.

In 1809 Drury Lane Theatre was destroyed by fire, and she retired from the stage – but not for long. Clarence was fourth in succession to the throne, after the Prince Regent, the Regent's daughter Princess Charlotte, and the childless Duke of York. If anything happened to the Princess, or she produced no children, the throne was likely to descend to Clarence, and he was under considerable pressure to marry, preferably a foreign princess, and produce an heir. Also he now fell in love with a beautiful young heiress, and in 1811 he yielded to these twin urgencies and, with affection and a generous settlement, he removed Mrs Jordan from his life.

She accepted with dignity this separation, which she had long feared was inevitable. For a little while she struggled on, acting again, though she was past her best and had lost her figure, and supporting, as she had always supported, her three elder daughters and their husbands, as well as her brothers and sister. Her allowance was not enough. '*Money, money, cruel money* [she wrote to Clarence], since my first setting out in the world at the age of thirteen, at a *moderate calculation* I have spun *fairly and honestly* out of my own brains above £100,000, and still this cruel *pelf* robs me of even comfort and *happiness*, as I verily believe we have nothing to do with our *own fate*. I may fairly say what a strange *one* mine has been, and *is likely to be*.' Her forecast was only too correct. She was always too loving and giving. She fell more and more into debt, and finally fled to France to escape her creditors. She died at St Cloud in 1816, under an assumed name, in solitude and penury, aged fifty-five.

[3]

In 1817 Princess Charlotte died, after giving birth to a stillborn son, and Clarence was one step nearer the throne. In 1818, after much indiscriminate and at times ridiculous wooing, he succeeded in marrying Princess Adelaide of Saxe-Meiningen, a dim but good woman who mended his manners and made him an excellent wife, without, however, producing a surviving heir. She went out of her way to be kind to the Fitzclarence children, but most of them showed little gratitude. An exception was the sixth child and third daughter Elizabeth. In 1814 Mrs Jordan described her as 'an extraordinary girl – and precisely *me* at *her* age'. In 1820 she married William George Hay, eighteenth Earl of Erroll: they were both nineteen. She and her husband lived with the Clarences at Bushy, and we are given glimpses of them by that splendid old gossip Thomas Creevey, who recorded that he and Lady Erroll 'became kind of cronies from the very first minute'.

Lady Erroll

At Christmas 1823 they attended the King's house-warming party at the Brighton Pavilion and had so much to eat that 'the fat Lady Erroll, who is a great dear, aches all over'. In 1827 Creevey wrote: 'What a handsome, spanking creature Lady Erroll is, and how like her mother, particularly when she used to be acting Nell [in *The Devil to Pay* by Charles Coffey]. She looks as if she was uncomfortable in her fine cloaths and wanted to have them off.' A year later Creevey found them in Dublin: 'Yesterday we had a nice domestic little snug party at the Errolls', in the Castle . . . and a very jubby day we had, Lady Erroll playing and singing her mother's kind of songs in the evening: the merits inferior I must admit to her divine original, and yet certainly like her; the whole to conclude with a game at fright.'

The Duke of York died in 1827, and King George IV in 1830. Clarence became King William IV, and soon after his accession he regularised the status of the Fitzclarences: the eldest son was given one of the King's subsidiary titles as Earl of Munster, and the others were awarded the style and precedence of the younger children of a marquess. Erroll was made an English peer and appointed Master of the Horse to Queen Adelaide. None of them showed any conspicuous gratitude, and despite the King's continued kindness and generosity they remained churlish and dissatisfied, with a chip of the bar sinister firmly on their shoulder. Munster made a scene when his application to carry the crown at the coronation was refused. But the Errolls stayed at court until the King's death in 1837.

The Errolls had four children, and in 1846 their second daughter, Lady Agnes Hay, married James Duff, who later succeeded his uncle as fifth Earl Fife. They were married in the British Embassy in Paris, where, exactly a hundred years later, their grandson was to rule as Ambassador. Duff had been in the diplomatic service and was now M.P. for Banffshire. He had the curious distinction of owning 250,000 acres in Morayshire, Banffshire, Aberdeenshire and Forfarshire, which at his death in 1879 were said to bring in £78,000 a year, but he owned no acres in Fife.

He was a natural recluse, with a horror of strangers, a trait that recurred in his daughter Agnes and other descendants. His grandson recorded:

It is recounted of him that having invited guests to luncheon in Scotland, his desire to see them would wane as the hour for their arrival approached. He would then instruct the butler to say he must have forgotten, as he had gone stalking, and he would retire to a spot on the hill whence he could spy the front door through his telescope, and would not come down until he had seen his friends drive away.

He and his wife lived mostly at Duff House, near Banff, which had been built by William Adam for the first Earl in the 1740s; and James

Imlach in his *History of Banff* (1868) describes how the tenantry and the citizens of Banff presented Lady Fife with her portrait by Sir Francis Grant, 'as a mark of the very high estimation in which the Countess is regarded by the numerous subscribers, for her charming condescension and affability, her great charity and consideration for the poor and afflicted over the wide family domain, with her unbounded hospitality and kindness to all who have the happiness of approaching her favoured and happy circle'.

Lady Fife by Sir Francis Grant

It was to this enviably circumstanced pair that, on 18 May 1852, at their London home in Eaton Place, was born their fifth child and fourth daughter, my future grandmother, Lady Agnes Cecil Emmeline Duff.

She was brought up largely at Duff House, and at the family's other country seat, Mar Lodge, near Braemar in Aberdeenshire. From nearby Abergeldie the Prince of Wales was a frequent visitor; the two families became great friends, and in 1889 the Prince's eldest daughter Princess Louise married the Fifes' only son, who was created first Duke of Fife.

Before long he was in danger of becoming consort to a future queen, for, with the death of Prince Eddy in 1891, only one precarious life stood between Princess Louise and the ultimate succession. But that life turned out to be a good one, and when Prince George recovered from typhoid, married his dead brother's fiancée Princess May of Teck, began to raise a family, and they stepped on to the stage as the future King George V and Queen Mary, the Fifes thankfully retired to the wings.

House party at Mar Lodge: Agnes in back row between her father (seated) and the Prince of Wales

The Duke was a heavy drinker – Max Beerbohm caricatured him in evening dress with a tartan face – and when Queen Victoria said to him 'I'm very glad, Lord Fife, to hear that you've given up port,' he replied, 'Yus, Marm, I find that whusky agrees with me better.'

Meanwhile his sister Agnes had grown up into a lively pretty girl with fair hair and blue eyes, and when she was nineteen she eloped with the twenty-two-year-old Viscount Dupplin, the handsome and dashing eldest son of the eleventh Earl of Kinnoull. Their daughter Marie Hay was born at Kinnoull Castle in 1873, but the marriage came to grief, and in April 1876 Agnes eloped again, this time with Herbert, younger brother of Cyril Flower, who was later the first Lord Battersea. Things moved quickly in those days. Dupplin divorced her in July, and she married Flower in August. He was undoubtedly the love of her life; they went round the world together, and lived blissfully for four years, until Flower died in 1880, aged twenty-seven.

Agnes was left with very little money; she was ostracised by Society because of her divorce; her daughter was in the so-called care of Dupplin; and her own family showed little sympathy. She decided she must do some kind of work, but she was trained for nothing. Hoping she might learn to become a nurse, she took a menial job in a London hospital. And here romantic legend must perhaps take the place of fact, though the two are often difficult to separate. A senior consulting surgeon, so they say, walking the wards, saw this lovely and still young woman scrubbing the floor, recognised her as the girl of his dreams, glimpsed in her childhood and never forgotten. She accepted his offer of marriage, and they lived happily ever after.

Alfred and Agnes Cooper in 1882

Certainly the last part of this account is true, for in 1882 Lady Agnes Flower married Mr Alfred Cooper, F.R.C.S. He was the son of a Norfolk barrister, had been educated at Merchant Taylors' School, trained at St Bartholomew's Hospital, and was now a very successful London surgeon: in 1865 he had, by operating, saved the life of an infant artist called Walter Sickert, who never forgot this benefaction. Alfred was fourteen years older than Agnes.

In 1874 he had been visiting a friend in St Petersburg at the time of the Duke of Edinburgh's wedding to the Tsar's daughter. The Prince of Wales fell ill, and Cooper was called in to doctor him. This led to a friendship with his future monarch, and to his knighthood in the Coronation Honours of 1902 (alongside Conan Doyle and Oliver Lodge). When he retired from St Mark's Hospital in 1899 his colleagues presented him with a clock 'as a slight recognition of the kindness, urbanity and zeal he displayed for thirty-four years whilst on the active staff of the hospital'.

In 1882 he and his wife settled down at 9 Henrietta Street, Cavendish Square, and there in the following year their daughter Stephanie (Steffie) was born. Hermione (Mione) followed in 1885, and then, on 26 November 1886, Lady Agnes was delivered of twins. It was a difficult birth: the boy-child was stillborn, and the girl, who weighed only $2\frac{3}{4}$ pounds, seemed unlikely to live. While doctor and midwife attended to her mother, this tiny great-great-granddaughter of Mrs Jordan was smothered in castor-oil, wrapped in cotton-wool, and left to fend for herself.

PART ONE : THE CHILD-WIFE

Come back into memory, like as thou went in the day-spring of thy fancies,
with hope like a fiery column before thee – the dark pillar not yet turned.

CHARLES LAMB

[1]

MIRACULOUSLY she survived and grew, and in due course she was
christened Sybil Mary. To her family this became Sibbie, but her own
first rendering of it as Biddie remained always her mother's, and later
my own, name for her.

As soon as she was old enough to be told about it, she mourned the
loss of her twin, and in later life she would sadly say that if he had lived
he might have given her some of the stability that she so often lacked.

When she was three years old her loss was mitigated by the birth of her
brother Duff. He at once became the pet of the family, and particularly
her pet; as they grew up they shared a passion for books, drama, and
especially poetry. In his autobiography *Old Men Forget* Duff described
himself as a spoilt and docile child, and of Sibbie he wrote:

> This youngest sister I loved deeply, and she had a great influence on
> my life. She was not an easy child to manage. She was wild and
> imaginative. She told me once that she was not my sister at all but that
> our parents had bought her out of a circus, a belief which I held for
> many years and which added romance to my affection.

When she was twelve, she and her sisters, having exhausted more than
one governess, were sent to school at nearby Queen's College in Harley
Street, from which Sibbie at least once played truant to see Ellen Terry in
a matinée, and Duff recorded how she came home for the summer
holidays

> possessed with the belief, strange and new to me, that it was a very
> good thing to be clever, and that the easiest way to become so was to
> read books, whether you understood them or not. We started straight

Sibbie and Duff

away with the plays of Shakespeare, distributing certain parts and taking the others alternately. We learnt duologues by heart – Brutus and Cassius, Romeo and Juliet, Hubert and Arthur, and the final meeting between Macbeth and Macduff. After we had recited this last one to my father we were told we had better forget it. Among some strong language, it refers to the circumstances of Macduff's birth, the result of a posthumous caesarian operation. Years afterwards, when we were both grown up and she was married, I asked her whether she remembered the day we gave our performance. 'Perfectly,' she said. 'Father had a most terrible cough and went behind that screen in the drawing-room.' 'Has it ever occurred to you,' I asked, 'that he was roaring with laughter?' It never had.

They also performed the quarrel on the moor from *Kidnapped* in what they believed to be Scottish accents, studied the theatrical columns in the papers, and, recalling their descent from Mrs Jordan, both determined to make the stage their profession. But at school Sibbie showed such a talent for languages that she was sent to a family in Brussels, whence she returned speaking fluent French with a perfect accent. Some years later she became equally proficient in Italian. In Belgium she was flattered but unmoved when a sixteen-year-old French boy called Robert Siegfried proposed marriage.

Mione, Steffie and Sibbie

Apart from Henrietta Street the family had another home. One of Alfred Cooper's friends and patients was the twelfth Duke of Hamilton, who owned all the Isle of Arran in the Firth of Clyde. As a wedding present he gave the Coopers four acres of land outside the village of Whiting Bay on the east coast of the island. There they built a spacious house of the local red sandstone, with a smaller one behind for the servants, and Duff Cottage for the gardener. The Duke was also Earl of Angus, and they named their house Cooper-Angus Lodge. There, beside the sea, and in the large garden where the Gulf Stream encouraged the growth of exotic plants, the children spent all their summer holidays, and for the rest of their lives they remembered the island with pleasure.

Two events were specially recalled in later years. One was Queen Victoria's Diamond Jubilee in 1897, when Lady Agnes refused to light the village bonfire in case she was expected to make a speech. The seven-year-old Duff deputised for her and was rather disappointed at not being asked to deliver what would have been the first of innumerable orations. The other occasion was the arrival of part of the Fleet in the neighbouring harbour of Lamlash, when the whole family was rowed out to lunch with Lord Charles Beresford on board his flagship.

The Coopers in their Arran garden

Sibbie grew up to be a beautiful girl, with her mother's blue eyes and golden hair. She was gay and generous and trustful, with a powerful desire for knowledge. By her seventeenth birthday she was outwardly adult; able, as always, to make immediate friends with anyone, regardless of age, sex, class, or nationality; precociously knowledgeable in language and literature; and extremely attractive to men. But beneath this assured appearance she was innocent and ignorant as few girls of her age are today. '*Notre destin est fait de nos hasards*', and by a chance encounter her future was fatally decided. Staying in a country house where licence was discreetly masked by the proprieties of the day, she was put in a bedroom next to that of a good-looking young man of twenty-five, who, assuming she was much older than seventeen and as experienced as she seemed to be, came through the communicating door and seduced her. His name was Richard Hart-Davis.

[2]

He was the son of a retired Captain of Engineers, and had won a scholarship to Eton, only to be removed under a cloud the following year: as his only surviving contemporary tactfully put it eighty years later, 'his particular schoolboy sensuality was considerably older than himself, so justice was indeed rough'. After some dismal trafficking with tutors and crammers he persuaded his father to indulge his undoubted musical gifts, and off he went to Leipzig to be trained as a professional pianist.

Although he found the continual practising tedious, he persevered for a considerable time and reached a standard high enough to afford himself pleasure for most of his life and to make him a popular performer in the houses of his friends, where he often accompanied Melba, Maggie Teyte, and later Richard Tauber. But there came a moment in his studies when he was forced to admit to himself that he would never be a second Paderewski, and was more likely to end up in a palm-court orchestra. So he sadly left Leipzig and returned to his parents, who were living near Limpsfield in Surrey.

For some time he hung about the house, disconsolately playing the piano, without plans or prospects, and then suddenly his future was assured by an extraordinary turn of fate. The neighbouring estate, Tandridge Court, was bought by a German-born financier called Max Michaelis, a partner in the firm of Wernher Beit, who, after twenty years' hard work, was reputed to have brought back eleven million pounds from the diamond-fields of South Africa.[1]

As was the custom, the Hart-Davises paid a ritual call on the newcomer, and in due course he returned the compliment. Desperate for some suitable topic of conversation, they asked Mr Michaelis if he was fond of music, and he, no doubt much relieved, said that he was. So Richard played the piano for him, and he was greatly taken with this handsome dark-haired young musician. He frequently asked the boy

[1] He later gave an art-library to Johannesburg and a fine collection of Dutch pictures (chosen by Hugh Lane) to Cape Town.

over to Tandridge, and then offered him a free fortnight at Monte
Carlo, whither he was taking some friends for Christmas.

Max Michaelis by Moses Kottler

A complete floor of the Hôtel de Paris was reserved for the Michaelis
party, and there Richard discovered that their host was suffering from an
extremely painful and disabling malady. When Richard visited his
benefactor each evening before dinner he invariably found him lying
down in some pain, the lights shaded, while across the room a valet
counted and piled up large numbers of *louis d'or* (in those days gambling
was done with real coins, not with chips). There was not a great deal for
the two of them to talk about, and, since gambling-money was not
included in Mr Michaelis's bounty, little for the boy to do while the rest
of the party were engrossed at the tables.

Monte Carlo was then the chief winter resort of all the *grandes cocottes*
of Europe, and that year the most beautiful and expensive of all these
multi-national *filles de joie* was known as Petits Pois, since she was said to
have about her person a number of tiny birthmarks of that size. At the
beginning of the second week of the Michaelis visit her lover of the
moment was called away on business, and wandering aimlessly through
the casino she spotted a good-looking boy gambling with francs in the
cheapest room, the Kitchen, picked him up and took him to her bed for
the rest of the week.

To the inexperienced Richard the whole episode was like something from the *Arabian Nights*, a crash-course in love-making with a ravishing professional teacher. But as the week drew all too quickly to an end he began to worry about Mr Michaelis's reactions, and sure enough, on the eve of their departure, when he paid his regular visit to the shaded room, Mr Michaelis said, in his heavy guttural English:

'I've noticed the company you've been keeping.'

'Yes, Mr Michaelis.'

'All I want to know is, how much have you been paying her?'

'Paying her? I haven't been paying her anything.'

'Do you mean to tell me that you have been living for a week with the most expensive woman in Europe without paying her anything?'

'Yes, Mr Michaelis.'

'In that case, my boy, I'll set you up in business for life.'

The idea of getting anything at so much below its market value overwhelmed Mr Michaelis, and he was as good as his word. When they got back to London he arranged for Richard to be taken on in a humble capacity by the stockbroking firm of Panmure Gordon, from which, some sixty years later, he retired as senior partner.

Nor was this the end of Mr Michaelis's benefactions. He introduced Richard to other South African millionaires, including Alfred Beit and particularly Lionel Phillips. This remarkable man, an English Jew, had made and lost two fortunes in South Africa, had taken part in the Jameson Raid, been sentenced to death, and reprieved in time to make a third fortune, which he was now enjoying. He and his extravagantly flamboyant wife Florence helped Richard financially and socially, took him on a cruise up the Nile (with a piano lashed to the deck of their paddle-steamer), to the Wagner festival at Bayreuth, and often invited him to their huge mock-Tudor mansion, Tylney Hall, near Basingstoke in Hampshire, where they employed seventy gardeners.

[3]

Such was the young man who broke into, and thereby ruined, Sibbie's life. He had met her briefly at the house of Mrs Norman Grosvenor, whose daughter Susan was a great friend of Sibbie's, and then arranged for her invitation to Tylney, where the seduction took place. No doubt he considered the episode a passing affair, but he had reckoned without Sibbie's innocence and romantic imagination. She was never truly in love with him, though for a short time she believed she was, but she was

Richard on the Nile

flattered and excited by his love-making, and thrilled to be thus unexpectedly inducted into womanhood. She believed that seduction inevitably resulted in pregnancy, she would love to have a child, and it seemed sensible to marry the child's father as soon as possible. Her sister Steffie had just been married, Mione was engaged: marriage was in the air.

Sibbie told her mother of her intention, and Lady Agnes, doubtless remembering the loves and excitements of her own turbulent youth, gave her blessing. But next day Sir Alfred revoked the benediction and forbade the marriage on the grounds of Sibbie's youth and their lack of money. If Sibbie had had any worldly wisdom or common sense she would have confided in her half-sister Marie Hay, who had just daringly set herself up in a London flat and started on her career as a writer.[1] She

[1] She published five historical monographs: *Diane de Poytiers*, 1900; *An Unrequited Loyalty* [Edward Somerset, Marquess of Worcester], 1901; *A German Pompadour* [Wilhelmine von Grävenitz], 1906; *The Winter Queen* [Elizabeth of Bohemia], 1911; and *Mas'aniello*, 1913: also *The Story of a Swiss Poet* [Gottfried Keller], 1920; and a ghostly novel, *The Evil Vineyard*, 1923. She married Herbert von Hindenburg, a diplomat and relation of the Field-Marshal, suffered greatly in Germany during the first war, and mercifully died before the second. She had no children.

Sibbie at Tylney

would certainly have advised caution and delay, with pertinent
questions: was Sibbie in fact pregnant? (she was not); had she and
Richard any tastes in common that would hold them together when the
excitement of their love-making waned? (they had not). But young
people seldom ask for advice unless they expect the right answer, and
Sibbie consulted no one. Richard was not averse from marrying his
attractive new conquest, defying parents was a novel excitement, and by
special licence the fatal wedding took place at St Mary Abbots,
Kensington, on 19 January 1904, when Sibbie was seventeen years and
two months old.

Buoyed up by hope and excitement they left for a five-day
honeymoon at the Hôtel de Lille et d'Albion in the Rue St Honoré in
Paris. From there Richard wrote to break the news to his elder sister
Madge:[1]

> Sybil has a divine childlike nature, and yet is very clever and well-read.
> She is tall and slight and very blonde, with a perfect figure and such
> pretty hands and feet, and lovely golden hair and clear candid eyes
> and the sweetest mouth and skin like satin. Isolde in fact to the life.

[1] For a brief account of Madge's life, see Appendix A, p. 147.

She has the most joyous nature and infectious laugh you ever heard, and it is impossible for anyone to be dull in her society.

To which Sibbie added:

I do so hope and pray that you will love me. Do you think you will? All my love to you, my sweet new sister.

Back in England they stayed briefly with Richard's maternal grandmother in Kensington and then travelled north to visit Richard's parents. His father, whose luck was always phenomenal, had, without any experience or qualifications, been appointed Chief Agent to the Earl of Ellesmere. With the job went a handsome salary and a half-timbered and moated Tudor house called Wardley Hall in the village of Worsley, near Manchester. Here Sibbie was received with affection, particularly by Madge, and the *fait accompli* of the marriage was immediately accepted.

At Wardley after the honeymoon

[4]

The Coopers also bowed to the inevitable and agreed to give Sibbie an allowance of £200 a year. Soon the young couple were dining at Henrietta Street and playing the newly popular game of bridge with their elders. Alfred Cooper had become slightly eccentric in his old age.

Bridge was played for love, but before the game started a footman was summoned to cover all the looking-glasses in the room, in case anyone might be tempted to cheat. If he thought a guest had stayed long enough, Sir Alfred rang for a footman and said, 'Fetch a hansom for Mr So-and-So.' He had never been a great reader, except of detective stories, of which he had amassed a large number, and he paid a considerable sum for Mr Bathurst of Bumpus's bookshop in London to travel to Arran to catalogue them. That was in the early years of this century, and I should dearly love to see those books – or even the catalogue.

Before long the young couple found a small house that they could afford: 79 Victoria Road, Kensington, in a cul-de-sac at the bottom of the street. At first the excitement of furnishing the house (to which Lionel Phillips and the Coopers' family friend Alfred Rothschild contributed liberally) and enjoying her new status as a married woman kept Sibbie busy and happy. She spent time learning to do her own hair, which she had never even tried to do before (in Paris they had been obliged to call in a *coiffeur*); she stumbled through the rudiments of housekeeping; tried in vain to keep cats out of the tiny back-garden; made new friends, and as always read every book she could lay hands on.

The Young Wife

[5]

Then gradually she began to realise her fatal mistake. Richard was not a bad man: many years later a gloomy butler, giving notice, perceptively said, 'Mr Hart-Davis is a good man at heart, but he's got me beat': certainly he was difficult for anyone – particularly Sibbie – to live with. He was extremely conventional and set in his ways, even at twenty-five, whereas Sibbie followed the gleam of her quicksilver mind, regardless of convention or taboo. Like Mrs Jordan she was a child of nature, and she was quite the wrong woman for Richard. To talk or play the piano to, he preferred women of title; as bedfellows the nearest he could get to Petits Pois. He could be very amusing in the right mood and company. He loved parties and was essentially worldly, whereas Sibbie was less sociable and preferred literary conversation to social chatter. He was intolerant of all who did not share his opinions, whereas Sibbie was always absorbed by a new idea or a fresh point of view.

Worst of all, perhaps because of his lack of formal education, Richard detested intellectuals, whom he invariably dismissed as 'priggish'. Sibbie was essentially an intellectual, and a great many of her future friends could be so described. And yet in his way Richard was an intelligent man: he always read a great deal, but in English only (he spoke a little French with an appalling accent, and a modicum of German from his Leipzig days), and though he took no interest in pictures, scenery, drama or architecture, he was extremely knowledgeable about music, for which Sibbie unfortunately had no ear. She was not quite so intolerant as her brother Duff, who, when asked whether he liked music, answered 'I prefer silence', but she found it hard to endure the volume of sound that she was condemned to hear during her married life.

Richard had a violent temper and was often brutally rude to waiters and other helpless underlings. This habit was hateful to Sibbie, to whom everyone was a sentient human being worthy of respect. All servants adored her and detested him.

She could never take the slightest interest in stockbroking or the City (an aversion which I inherited), and would have agreed with the younger Dumas, who, when asked to define business, said: '*C'est bien simple: c'est l'argent des autres.*'

Then there were the financial problems. Sibbie had been brought up, as later I was by her, with little ready money but with a firm belief (often severely tested) that in an emergency enough could be obtained from somewhere. Richard was reticent and cheese-paring about money. Never to her dying day had Sibbie the faintest idea of how much he earned in the City, what they could afford, or what would be doled out for her own spending, above her family's allowance of £200 a year. Perhaps this was just as well, since whenever she was given any money she immediately spent it or gave it away – the Mrs Jordan blood again.

Reluctant to part with small sums for any purpose, Richard never grudged paying the maximum for three things: trains, hotels, and telegrams. Whenever Sibbie went anywhere by train he gave her the money for her first-class fare, and she invariably went third class, spending the difference on books to read on the way. This habit he never began to understand. He was reasonably fond of her in his way, but his way was not her way. The marriage-tie, and later the children, held them together, but increasingly they led their separate lives.

[6]

Later in 1904 Sibbie fell ill with suspected appendicitis, but recovered sufficiently to see Duff almost every day during his Christmas holidays from Eton. Then and at the following Easter they indulged their old love of the theatre, seeing the latest plays – Barrie's *Peter Pan* and *Alice-Sit-by-the-Fire*, Shaw's *Candida* and *John Bull's Other Island*, the first revival of *Lady Windermere's Fan*, and many other dramas of less consequence. Sibbie and Richard went often to concerts and operas. In one holiday they took Duff to Tylney for the week-end, and Sibbie persuaded him to read aloud Meredith's 'Love in the Valley' in the crowded drawing-room. She enjoyed it so much that she immediately asked him to read it again, which he happily did, to the agonised boredom of the other guests.

During the next two years Sibbie acquired a large number of new men-friends, including several passionate admirers. How many of them were technically her lovers is impossible to know, for she was as generous in love as in everything else, but certainly the most important of them at this time was Gervase Beckett, brother of the second Lord Grimthorpe. He was a Yorkshire banker, married with four daughters, and in 1906, the year in which Sibbie met him, he became Unionist Member of Parliament for Whitby. He was twenty years older than Sibbie.

Their love-affair certainly lasted for two years, during which Sibbie was a constant visitor at Beckett's Yorkshire homes, first Kirkstall

Duff and Sibbie in Victoria Road

Grange, near Leeds, and then Kirkdale Manor, near Helmsley. On one occasion they ran away to Paris together, and a friend had to be sent to fetch them back. Richard, who sometimes accompanied Sibbie to Yorkshire, must have known what was going on, but he seems to have ignored it.

In Yorkshire: Sibbie

In Yorkshire: Sibbie and Gervase Beckett

In Yorkshire: Sibbie and Gervase Beckett

In Yorkshire: Picnic on the Moors (Two Beckett daughters, Sibbie, Mrs Beckett, Richard)

At Duncombe Park, very near Kirkdale, lived Beckett's sister-in-law by marriage, Marjorie (always known as Queenie), Viscountess Helmsley. She was a daughter of the famous Lady Warwick, and was later to be Beckett's second wife and the mother of his son Martyn. Queenie and Sibbie became devoted friends, read poetry together, and called each other Undine and Tiger Lily. Another friend in the family was Beckett's nephew Ralph, later the third Lord Grimthorpe. Sibbie was still visiting Yorkshire as late at 1913.

Back in London there were other excitements, other lovers. She enjoyed herself immensely, and when she found she was pregnant she felt overjoyed and completely fulfilled. Lovingly she made every preparation, and at 6.15 on the morning of 28 August 1907, when she was still three months short of her twenty-first birthday, I was born at 79

Victoria Road. This was a double turning-point in her life. On the one hand it presented her with a being who was hers alone, on whom she could lavish her overflowing affection in the certainty of being equally loved in return, but on the other hand it tied her for ever to the husband with whom she had so little in common.

Mother and son 1907

INTERLUDE ON PATERNITY

It is a wise father that knows his own child.
LAUNCELOT GOBBO

I AM REASONABLY certain that, biologically speaking, Richard Hart-Davis was not my father, but, as John Gore neatly put it, 'when paternity is in doubt, certainty is hard to attain'. And when the mother herself is uncertain who fathered her children, as my mother told Duff she was, nothing is left but fascinating conjecture. My sister's paternity is as questionable as mine, and through the years we have spent many happy hours discussing the possibilities, hoping that perhaps we had the same father, until with age we have come to realise that it

'avails thee not
To whom related, or by whom begot'.

To begin with, the Hart-Davis family were almost all short, stocky and dark-haired. My sister and I were tall and slim and fair. We may have inherited all these characteristics from our mother, but in childhood we disliked Richard so much, because of his insensitive and sometimes brutal treatment of our mother, that, long before we knew of any foundation for our belief, we enjoyed quoting these discrepancies as evidence that he was not our real father.

There were several candidates for that post, including a fair-haired Spanish grandee, but in later years we gradually, on various grounds, eliminated all but two. One of these was a man called Lionel Bulteel: he was certainly our mother's lover at the requisite time, and she once said that he might possibly have fathered both of us. I never saw him until 1937, when I was delighted to receive a note from the Marylebone Cricket Club, saying that he had put me down when I was born and that I was now eligible for membership. Excited by this clue, and because there was some paper he had to sign, I wrote and asked if I might see him.

Our interview took place in a very dark room in the Turf Club, but it was just light enough for me to perceive that he was of smallish stature, with no resemblance to my sister or myself. I told him of my great love of cricket and thanked him profusely for proposing me for the M.C.C., but when I attempted to speak of my mother he remained sternly uncommunicative. He may in 1907 (and even in 1937) have suspected that he might be my father, but if so he was determined not to discuss the matter. I thanked him again, he signed the paper, and I took my leave, feeling sure that I was not his son. I never saw him again.

The other, and much stronger, candidate was Gervase Beckett, whom I never saw after those early Yorkshire years.[1] He was tall, passionately interested in books, pictures and other beautiful objects, and a great devotee of cricket. I harp on this game because my own fervent and lifelong interest in it was certainly not inherited from the Cooper or Hart-Davis families (who all detested it), nor from my own cricketing prowess, which was mediocre. I discovered later that Ger Beckett (as he was called by his family and friends) was gay and amusing in company, but liked to get away from it all – a trait which has always been strong in my own nature. Again the dates fitted, but the only two surviving letters from Ger to my mother are gay but guarded, and we found nothing more to further our theory until chance took a hand.

One day in 1962 I was having a pre-lunch drink in the crowded bar of the Garrick Club, when Martyn Beckett came into the room. He had never seen me before, didn't know who I was, and could see nothing but my silhouette against a window. Directly he saw it he stopped suddenly and said, 'By God, that's my father!' It appeared that I was roughly the same height as his father and was standing in an attitude that was particularly his. This surely was clinching evidence. Martyn and I have discussed the matter at length and happily agree that we are half-brothers. His elder half-sister Prue has likewise lovingly accepted me into her family. Later still I saw a good deal of Eve Fairfax, that same friend who had been sent to Paris to fetch the lovers home. She was by now in her late nineties (she lived to be 106) but all her faculties were still sharp. 'You look more like Ger every day,' she several times said. And when I finally came to live in Yorkshire I felt, although my village is fifty miles from Kirkdale, that in some mysteriously instinctive way I was coming home.

Be all that as it may, Richard Hart-Davis, with whatever doubts and

[1] He was made a baronet in 1921 and died in 1937.

misgivings, accepted me as his son, gave me his name, paid for my upkeep and education, and in every way treated me well, according to his lights. He was the only father I ever knew, I owe him a great deal, and I shall refer to him as my father during the rest of this narrative.

PART TWO : THE YOUNG MOTHER

In the dark womb where I began
My mother's life made me a man.
Through all the months of human birth
Her beauty fed my common earth.
I cannot see, nor breathe, nor stir,
But through the death of some of her.

JOHN MASEFIELD

[1]

FROM THE moment of my birth I was cherished, cosseted, pampered and thoroughly spoiled for the rest of my mother's life. She breast-fed me for nine months, letting nothing interfere, leaving any dinner-party for my ten-o'clock feed, and she largely looked after me herself, though I was technically in the charge of a nanny. She put on considerable weight after my birth but soon retracted to her accustomed slimness. Sixty years later her friend Susan Grosvenor (by then Tweedsmuir) told me:

> I remember meeting her in Oxford Street, pushing you in a pram. She told me that she had made up her mind not to bother about clothes, and also that she was going to all sorts of interesting places in London to hear sermons and lectures. I can see her now in a neat grey suit with a not new fox-fur round her neck, looking charming as she always did.

If I immediately became, and ever remained, the still centre of her somewhat unstable universe, she was certainly always the whole extent of mine. Hazlitt's words about Mrs Jordan exactly describe my mother in my earliest memory: 'her person was large, soft, and generous like her soul . . . all gaiety, openness and good nature . . . nothing dexterous or knowing about her . . . the child of nature'. The joy of her presence never waned, and I can perfectly understand why so many men fell in love with her. She was 'of imagination all compact', and her gift of saying and doing the unexpected made her an entrancingly exciting companion.

[2]

When, towards the end of 1908, she again became pregnant, it was clear that Victoria Road would be uncomfortably crowded with two children, so the family moved across the Park to a larger house, 3 Stanhope Street, Lancaster Gate. This was convenient for my father's daily journey to the City by underground, and on the edge of Hyde Park and Kensington Gardens, in which we made pilgrimages to the Round Pond and the Albert Memorial. The smell of hawthorn-blossom always takes me back affectionately to those early days.

The new house demanded a larger staff, and to improve her Italian my mother engaged a lady's maid called Emma Lorenzoni and a genial giant of a butler called Eugenio Capuggi, who won my heart by repeatedly carrying me out into the street and letting me drop used electric-light bulbs into the area, where they exploded with most satisfying reports. He fell in love with our red-haired housemaid Nellie, and though their assignations often went awry owing to their inability to speak each other's language, they eventually married. My father, who had no Italian, spoke to Capuggi in his atrocious French, which the poor man usually failed to understand. At the outbreak of war Capuggi took Nellie with him and went home to Italy to enlist. A year or two later he came to visit us in the London hotel where we were staying, resplendent in his grey-green army uniform; he survived the war and came to see my mother in 1921 when I was away at school, bringing a green parrot for my sister. Emma also stayed with us till August 1914, and was then taken over by my Aunt Steffie. I have often wondered why my mother made no effort to bring up my sister and myself to be at least bilingual, but the idea seems not to have occurred to her.

Even with so many servants she found housekeeping irksome. Every week my father made her enter into a notebook the names of all the regular tradesmen and the amount of their weekly bills. Once she wrote 'Yah! these beastly household books!' in the margin, and sometimes to relieve the tedium she set out the names in Greek characters.

The house had four storeys and a basement. There was a large L-shaped drawing-room on the first floor and a similar bedroom for my mother above. There, on 5 July 1909, my sister Deirdre was safely born. She was beautiful from birth, and whatever my father's misgivings about her paternity, she quickly became his pet and favourite. He was tolerably fond of children, particularly when they were small. I was bitterly jealous of the baby, resented my mother's paying her so much attention, and temporarily bore a grudge against the good man who had delivered her: 'Rupert threw his little hansom cab at Dr Easton', recorded my mother. Nevertheless he remained our doctor until the war, after which we were looked after by Dr E. P. Furber, a jovial man of great kindness, skill and shrewd common sense.

Sibbie and her children

[3]

Meanwhile Sibbie's brother Duff was at Oxford, and many of his friends and contemporaries there, that generation so soon to perish, became friends and admirers of hers. Among them were John Manners, Denis Anson, Edward Horner, Edward (Bimbo) Tennant, Billy Grenfell, and most particularly Patrick Shaw-Stewart and, of a slightly older generation, Raymond Asquith.

Raymond, the eldest son of the Prime Minister, was eight years older than Sibbie. He had won every possible scholastic honour – scholarships to Winchester and Balliol, the Craven, Hertford and Derby scholarships, Firsts in Mods, Greats, and Law, and a Fellowship at All Souls. In 1907 he had married Katharine Horner, and now he was reading for the Bar. After his death John Buchan wrote of his 'great beauty of person', and went on: 'I have never met anyone so endowed with diverse talents . . . His wit flowed as easily as a brook, and into curious eddies . . . Someone, in one of the round games which were then popular, propounded a stupid riddle: "What is that which God never sees, kings rarely see, and we see every day?" The answer is "An equal". Raymond's answer was "A joke".'

He was a brilliant parodist. His 'Lines addressed to a Viscount who died Young', in the style of Tennyson's *In Memoriam*, contain this quatrain:

> We met, we spoke, we laugh'd, we talk'd –
> We spoke but common words and few;
> I told you of an Earl I knew,
> You said you thought the wine was cork'd.

'In Praise of Young Girls', in the style of Pope, stresses the speed of the modern seductress, compared to that of the Mona Lisa:

> Our modern maiden smears the twig with lime
> For twice as many hearts in half the time.
> Long ere the circle of that staid grimace
> Has wheeled your weary dimples into place,
> Our little Chloe (mark the nimble fiend)
> Has raised a laugh against her bosom friend,
> Melted a Marquis, mollified a Jew,
> Kissed every member of the Eton crew,
> Ogled a Bishop, quizzed an aged peer,
> Has danced a Tango and has dropped a tear.

Patrick Shaw-Stewart, who was two years younger than Sibbie, came of a Scottish military family. Academically he was almost Raymond's equal, with Eton and Balliol scholarships, the Hertford, the Ireland, Firsts in Mods and Greats, and an All Souls Fellowship. After Oxford he turned to business, joined the merchant bankers Baring Brothers, and when war broke out in 1914 he was managing director at the age of twenty-six.

Under the influence of two such phenomenal classical scholars Sibbie began to learn Greek with Janet Case[1] and was soon able to enjoy reading with a lexicon beside her. Patrick advised her which bits of Aeschylus's *Prometheus Bound* to tackle, Raymond helped her with Plato, especially the *Crito*. This exercise satisfied some of her thirst for knowledge and she persisted in it with determined concentration. She also went to many lectures, and set herself reading-courses in English, French, and Italian literature. She would have loved a university.

For the rest, she saw a great deal of Duff when he was in London, and of her mother, to whom she was always devoted. They went to many theatres, particularly enjoying Tree's productions of *Trilby* and *An Enemy of the People*, and Pélissier's *Follies*. She took us children to stay at Tylney and at Kirkdale, and entertained modestly in her new home.

[4]

Then in November 1909, leaving us to nanny and nurserymaid, she set off on a six-week visit to France and Italy with her mother and Duff, whose brief journal of the tour has survived. They began with a week at the Hôtel Meurice in Paris, where they dutifully saw the sights. In Notre Dame, Sibbie bought and set up a candle, perhaps to an unknown God, but she always loved the lights, warmth and colour of Catholic churches. Once, when they had climbed to the top of a lofty tower, Duff couldn't resist trying to drop their *Baedeker* on to a man who was using a *pissoir* far below. He missed, and Lady Agnes was greatly puzzled. 'What *has* darling Duffy done with the *Baedeker*?' And that essential volume had to be replaced. They also went to as many theatres as possible, seeing Lucien Guitry in Bernstein's *La Griffe* and Sarah Bernhardt in *L'Aiglon*, as well as the Grand Guignol and other plays.

Next they spent three days at Montreux in Switzerland, visiting Chillon, Les Avants and Glion, before moving on to Milan, which they reached on the eve of Sibbie's twenty-third birthday. A day's sight-seeing there, and then to Florence, where they spent a fortnight. Brother and sister arranged Italian lessons for themselves, visited many churches and galleries, and every evening read Motley's *Rise of the Dutch Republic* aloud. At luncheon with Lady Paget at Bellosguardo they met Henry Labouchere and his wife, later lunching with them in their villa. On 8

[1] This remarkable woman also taught Virginia Woolf, whose obituary tribute to her is printed as Appendix B on p. 149.

December Duff chronicled: 'To Santa Maria del Carmina in rain. Sibbie would go on and see another church, but went alone. She loves churches, I hate them.'

Then came a fortnight at the Hôtel Regina in Rome: more Italian lessons, much more sight-seeing, with visits to Tivoli, the Villa d'Este, the graves of Keats and Shelley. On 16 December Duff recorded: 'To the Forum in perfect weather. After lunch Sibbie and I childishly quarrelled and threw coffee and things at one another. We then went to the Vatican and made it up on the way.' One day they went for a lovely drive in the country, reciting poetry to each other all the way.

Back to Paris, where they saw Polaire in *La Maison de Danse*, which Duff described as 'a very thrilling, very beautiful play'. Then Richard joined them, and on New Year's Eve they supped at Abbaye: 'We had engaged a table in the upstairs room, as none was to be had below. Richard was furious at first, because, contrary to my advice, and in accordance with his own wishes, we arrived too soon and the room was completely empty. He soon warmed to his work however and danced quite madly with the girls. Sibbie also seemed perfectly happy.' Next day they walked in the Bois and went to 'a quite good farce, but Richard hated it and swore all the time'. Two days later they were back in London.

[5]

Except for a few scattered pages in later years, the only diaries of Sibbie's that have survived are those for 1910 and 1911. They record books read and lectures attended, daily Italian lessons, much riding in Rotten Row and the country, constant self-exhortation, undeserved self-reproach for intellectual idleness, and already the deadening insomnia from which she was never to be free. Here are a few early entries for 1910:

7 Feb Tried to write two essays [inspired by reading Hazlitt]. Fearful fiasco. There is absolutely nothing in the world that I can do the least bit well, yet, pathetically, I always (although I should of course deny it if publicly asked) feel that I am rather a splendid person, and in a vague indefinite way immeasurably clever.

3 March Trying to give up smoking. Failed ignominiously.

4 March Felt wretched. No sleep all night. To Wallace Collection and lecture on Baudelaire.

8 March   Lunched with Keyserling – delightful; told me about the Chartreux monks, how they looked like snow on the ground when prostrated in the church.

9 March   Slept well with aid of veronal. To lecture by W. B. Yeats – thrilling.

21 March   I want every day to have seen something beautiful, have acquired some knowledge, and been kind.

22 March   Dined Ritz – G[er] B[eckett], Queenie, Richard. To *The Madras House.*

Among new friends of this time were the poet Alice Meynell, her literary journalist husband Wilfrid, and their children, who were to play an important part in my later life. Their youngest son Francis recorded how in 1910 he was sent, as substitute for his father, to a dinner-party at Stanhope Street, where he met Duff, Lady Diana Manners, Eddie Marsh, the twittering Maecenas of his day, and Lady Tree, the witty actress wife of the actor-manager Herbert Beerbohm Tree. She became a close friend of Sibbie's, and even more so did her daughters, Viola, Felicity and Iris. Tree's half-brother Max Beerbohm told me years later that he had first seen me in a pram in my parents' hall.

Iris was only thirteen in 1910, but despite the ten-year difference in their ages she and my mother became lifelong friends. Beautiful, gifted as poet, actress and linguist, Iris was a true Bohemian, with a positive love of unconventionality, a delight in natural behaviour, indifferent to money, comfort or accepted standards of conduct. Whenever she and my mother talked of matters unsuitable for my infant years, they spoke in French and Iris would say, 'Yes, Rupert, we're talking about you.' As children we always welcomed her appearance because one never knew what she might say or do next. She loved scandalising the conventional, particularly my father, who disapproved of her way of living, but could not help liking and being amused by her. On one occasion, as they were walking down a village street in Kent, Iris saw an empty butcher's cart, leaped into the driving-seat and whipped the horse into a canter; at Brighton she walked chin-deep into the sea fully dressed, and my father had to escort her dripping back to the Metropole Hotel.

Back in London the diary continued:

24 May   Rupert looks so full of health and vigour, and passing fair withal. I am glad I nursed him and helped to make him what he is.

Iris Tree by Augustus John

10 July 'And I dared to grow wild again with these various and shadowy loves' (St Augustine).

30 July I want to become more profound. I rather hate frivolous people – really frivolous all through, I mean. I have a sore throat and the music that goes on all the time is a bore.

For the summer holidays we children were despatched with our attendants to a little rented house at Westgate-on-Sea, where my mother visited us regularly until in September she and Richard went to stay with the Grimthorpes in their fabulously situated Villa Cimbrone, near Ravello.

The moment she got back to London:

8 Oct Have been to the children's bedside. Both fast asleep. My heart goes out to them. I will do all I can for them, now and always, my darlings.

9 Oct Deirdre has great charm, and is rather like the picture of the *Roi de Rome*.

*With the grandparents at
Wardley*

And then she came up against two perennial problems:

23 Oct   Don't quite understand about Ireland. Must find out about
it.

9 Nov   I am always hearing of the sins of other people, told me in
horror and *astonishment*. Yet most of us go to church avowing all to be
miserable sinners, so why so much surprise over every sin?

[6]

On New Year's Day 1911 we were all at Kirkdale Manor, and Sibbie
had begun to translate the Abbé Dimnet's recently published book *Les
Soeurs Brontë*. Then in London:

21 Jan   Wasted afternoon pottering about after spiritualists.

23 Jan   Went to see the Suggestor – a curious, rather interesting old
man, no appearance of charlatanism. Am to start treatment
tomorrow.

25 Jan To Suggestor again. Steffie says 'God is a man of about thirty-two'. (Steffie is twenty-seven.)

28 Jan Must try and read less if necessary, but *think about* and *digest* better what I read. I am always in such a hurry to get on, like a traveller journeying at full speed so as to see all, but going so fast that he hardly sees anything. Steffie is always saying that I shall one day become a saint. Alas! I fear me never. At best I should be like Lamb's description of Coleridge – a damaged archangel!

3 Feb Spent morning doing the Brontë book.

5 Feb To City Temple, Campbell has tremendous magnetism and never fails to stimulate me.

22 Feb Duff's twenty-first birthday. To Chelsea Arts Ball. Danced with John Manners, Denis Anson etc. Almost daylight when I came home. [For one such dance she ordered a gold pierrot dress, with a mask, and told all her friends about it. Five minutes before the ball began she persuaded Duff to exchange it for his black pierrot dress, thus ensuring a full night's comedy of errors.]

26 Feb Am haunted by the idea of old age creeping on one. It seems to me I always look so old nowadays – storm-beaten – and am almost continuously tired.

27 Feb It is so difficult to disentangle threads in life; they will stick together.

5 March Tea with the Meynells. She said Francis Thompson saw a resurrection in every sunrise and a crucifixion in every sunset.

7 March Wilfrid Meynell came for two and a half hours – a pure delight. Reading poems to me and bringing an atmosphere in which the spirit seems to be set free. 'All the poets,' he said, 'almost without exception, did not care for music.'

5 April 'Unstable as water . . . too loving of love . . . too understanding of another's heart's desire . . . too quick to grant . . . too quick to take away.'

At the end of April she went for a month to Fontainebleau, whence she often spent the day in Paris. There she saw something of the Abbé Dimnet, who was a great Anglophile. He took her to the Louvre and introduced her to the artist Charles Huard, who illustrated the big Conard edition of Balzac. 'He was so charming. I delight in him.' He proved also to be a friend of Ger Beckett's.

18 May   Paris for the day. Lunch and tea with the Huards. I said I should like to live alone in the country. '*Ah*,' said he, '*c'est un bon rêve qu'on se fait.*'

24 May   Paris. Tea with the Abbé. Delightful long talk. He thought my essay bad and told me so, as I had hoped he would.

And then came the usual happy reunion:

27 May   To London. Quite a rapture seeing the children again – both so fair. Deirdre has sweet shy eyes. Rupert of course is marvellous.

The children growing up

The summer was spent between Tylney and the seaside, and then the diary is blank, except for another brief visit to Kirkdale, where Charles Huard and the sculptor John Tweed were fellow-guests. They visited Castle Howard, and then the majestic ruin of Rievaulx Abbey. 'Huard said that if it belonged to him he would ride up and down it naked on a white horse with golden shoes and a green saddle.' He also told her that his idea of heaven was a tall tower lined with books from top to bottom, in which he would live in a wall-less room like a lift, in telephonic communication with the best Paris restaurants.

3 Sept Took *Clayhanger* into C.H. *Nous nous tutoyons maintenant!* Looked at engravings of Old Masters with Ger. Mark Sykes arrived for lunch and did amusing imitations – so clever: *pétillant d'esprit.* Dressed up for dinner, I and C.H. as Apaches, Tweed as Friar Tuck.

11 Sept Rupert can pronounce his h's. Great triumph. He is awarded sixpence.

On the day after her twenty-fifth birthday she accompanied her mother for a week to Paris, where she saw more of the Huards, and this comparatively untroubled year ended with Christmas at Tylney.

[7]

1912 brought friendship with the painter William Nicholson and his family. They were living at Rottingdean, near Brighton, and my parents took a little house there for the summer holidays, so that Nicholson could paint a picture of Deirdre and me sitting on a piano.

Duff came to stay and reported to his mother:

Rupert and Deirdre by William Nicholson

I am so sorry I haven't written before but there is only one writing-table in the house, and that being in the dining-room I hadn't discovered it till now. Richard has gone away this morning, but not before I had relieved him of £3 at double dummy. I have been sleeping here all right as they have a little spare room if they make one of the servants sleep out. Sibbie wants you to come down here and told me to ask you. I think you would love the place but am not sure you'd be any too comfortable . . . I like the picture of the children very much but am not sure whether you will. It isn't at all flattering of them. The weather here is too heavenly this morning and we are just going for a ride.

Sibbie immediately made great friends with Nicholson's wife Mabel, always called Prydie since she was a sister of James Pryde, the painter who had collaborated with Nicholson as The Beggerstaff Brothers, designing posters and woodcuts. In the autumn Sibbie and Prydie spent a month together in Paris, first at the Hôtel du Quai Voltaire and then in a *vie-de-Bohème* studio, where Prydie painted a fine head of Sibbie, while Sibbie made further efforts towards self-expression.

Sibbie by Mabel Pryde Nicholson

She longed to write something creative, but Ger Beckett dissuaded her:

You must not write a novel yet: you don't know enough and have not 'taken in' sufficiently. You have plenty of time and must use it in learning and recording. You receive impressions and experience feelings, but you don't use either to a literary end. You plunge into the sea of life but you don't learn to swim. There are things you must acquire and things you must leave behind, and what they are you must find out if you can. Meanwhile you must write and write and write, and burn and burn and burn. So much for turning me into a moral lecturer.

Instead she planned to translate Synge's *Playboy of the Western World* into French – a daunting task indeed – but luckily the rights were not available, and she was reduced to struggling on with *Les Soeurs Brontë*, somewhat chastened by its author:

Mais quand donc ferons-nous paraître la traduction de ce petit livre dont vous vous occupiez il y a un an ou deux? La vie est courte, petite Sybille, hâtons-nous. Non, ne nous hâtons pas, vous avez raison. Mais faisons les choses une à la fois et quand nous les commençons, finissons les. C'est le résidu de ma sagesse acquise et c'est déjà beaucoup.

She had translated a good deal of the work before the pressure of events stopped the flow, and the book did not appear in English until 1924, when it had another translator. In Paris Sibbie was persuaded by Lady Phillips to sit to the Russian sculptor Naoum Aronson as a model for the head of the Angel of Peace that surmounts the towering Johannesburg Memorial to the Rand Regiments who fought for the British in the Boer War.

[8]

In the early summer of 1913 Sibbie suffered some sort of illness or breakdown, for which she was ordered a rest-cure. This she took on a day-bed in the L-alcove of her Stanhope Street bedroom. Despite the bedside telephone and any number of books and visitors, she found the inactivity wearisome. William Nicholson came often to see her. He was always fascinated by the way she could bend her fingers backwards – said to be a sign of great generosity – and sent her a drawing to emphasise his admiration.

Letter from William Nicholson

When he said he would like to paint her portrait *in situ* she eagerly agreed. He explained that he could not afford to work for nothing, and that his fee would be £500. 'You needn't worry about that,' she said; 'Richard will gladly pay for it,' so next day the picture was begun. But when Richard returned tired and irritable from the City he immediately asked how much the picture was going to cost. Seeing her entertainment slipping away, she impulsively told him Nicholson was doing it for nothing. And so the painting continued, and knowledge of the inevitable dénouement cannot have hastened the patient's recovery. When the dreaded day arrived, she summoned Richard and Nicholson to her bedside and said: 'Everything I've told you for the past weeks has been a lie.' The ensuing row reverberated for months. All right was on the painter's side, and he threatened either to remove the picture or sue for payment. Eventually he agreed to accept £150 if they would return his landscape 'The Brighton Road', which he had given them. Relations between the two families were never the same again, but years later I saw a great deal of Nicholson and he was extremely good to me.

Sibbie by William Nicholson

By the end of July Sibbie was well enough to go to Diana Manners's ball in Arlington Street, and a few days later she wrote to Iris Tree from Westgate-on-Sea:

I have just had two ghastly days quite alone in this pretty bloody hotel, not world-forgetting but by the world forgot. On Tuesday I join the children in their little house. Rupert has a room to himself there, with a text over his bed: Lord Remember Me. 'Remember *who?*' he keeps asking.

Later in August she stayed a few days with the Horners at Mells in Somerset, but, despite the presence of Raymond Asquith, Patrick Shaw-Stewart and Edward Horner, she wrote to Iris: 'I miss Rupert a good deal and I shan't see him for six weeks. Do write and tell me nice, kind, gentle things, please.'

Mells 1913: Raymond Asquith and Patrick Shaw-Stewart

At Kirkdale Manor there were some compensations. 'It is quite fun here,' she told Iris. 'There is a girl of sixteen who worships the ground I tread on: Millions of dead grouse to eat: a lovely house: wonderful long-tailed Arab ponies to ride on purple moors: Members of Parliament who hang on my words. Every evening I win little piles of sovereigns at bridge with F. E. Smith, and the sun is shining. And yet, "tired with all these", for you, ill-mannered, freckled and much too fat, I yearn.'

And then from Venice in September:

This morning I am more unhappy than most days. I have been lying sobbing on the smiling sand for an hour. I hate everyone in the world at this moment except you. Richard is so brisk and sensible. I am a fool, darling. I stand on the edge of life and throw pebbles into the sea. It would be better to throw myself in and have done with it. My brain is like the worst sort of switchback; I am always either in a dull, disappointing hell or in a silly swaying heaven. Venice has been a long agony to me. When I am in a madhouse, pretty, will you bring me fresh straws for my hair?

But there were moments of pleasure: 'Dennie Anson has taught me to swim under water and I can do it for miles. Nothing easier.' And then Duff reported to his mother:

Last night there was a wonderful fancy dress ball. Sibbie and Richard came with our party. At the end of the ball, i.e. about 3 a.m., the whole party went to the Piazza and danced there. The hostess, a lady called Marchesa Casati, appeared on the Piazza with very few clothes and a parrot on her shoulder, leading a leopard and followed by two black boys.

Ronald Storrs remembered meeting Sibbie at such a party, and how they escaped from the hurly-burly and recited Meredith's poetry to each other in a gondola.

Back in London, during a further period of rest-cure in November, Sibbie wrote to Iris:

I have drunk some wine today and William Nicholson has been finishing my portrait. Raymond has been again to see me. I am happy, and in my heart are dozens of late larks twittering like hell.

[9]

The fatal year 1914 opened gaily. A few extracts from Duff's diary
and letters set the scene for January:

> Dined at the Savoy with the Raymond Asquiths, Sibbie, and Patrick
> [Shaw-Stewart]. They went afterwards to *The Doctors' Dilemma*, where
> Diana and Iris Tree were waiting for them.
>
> Played bridge at Foreign Office with Patrick, Sibbie and Raymond.
>
> To Alhambra, where I found Patrick and Sibbie. Had supper with
> them at Gambrinus.
>
> Dinner at Dieudonné – Katharine [Asquith], Raymond, Ego and Letty
> Charteris [Diana's sister], Sibbie, John Manners and Felicity Tree.
> They went afterwards to *The Silver Box* and back to supper at Bedford
> Square [the Asquiths' home].
>
> First night of the revised *Darling of the Gods* at His Majesty's. Alan and
> Viola Parsons (*née* Tree) and Iris Tree were there. Sibbie and Richard
> and Lady Tree joined them.
>
> Lunched with Sibbie, Iris Tree and Denis Anson. Dined at Carlton
> Grill with Sibbie, Iris, Alan and Viola, to whose house we went back
> afterwards. Read Sir Thomas Browne's *Urn Burial* to them till they
> were all asleep.
>
> I hear Sibbie has cut all her hair off.

She was the first in their circle to take this revolutionary step, but Iris and
others soon followed. She wore her hair short for the rest of her life. And
then in February:

> Lunched at 3 Stanhope Street. Sibbie, Richard, Raymond and Mrs
> Patrick Campbell.
>
> Dined with Sibbie and Richard. Cynthia and Beb [Herbert] Asquith
> were there, Evelyn Fitzgerald and Cuckoo Belleville, Max Beerbohm
> and Mrs Patrick Campbell. We had a very good dinner and played
> poker afterwards.

And so it went on. Soon after this she was almost certainly the first
woman to loop the loop in an aeroplane. This she did with the dashing
Swedish airman Gustav Hamel in an open two-seater machine with
simple straps over her shoulders. She found it exhilarating and felt no
fear. Later in the year Hamel was drowned when his plane crashed in the
sea. Duff wrote a poem in his memory, which was published in *The Times*.

And then comes the first mention of the greatest love of her life, the man who was the cause of so much joy and anguish, the man she loved more than any other. On 24 March Duff wrote to his mother: 'Sibbie's latest admirer is Sidney Herbert. He says he adores her.' He was the elder son of the Hon. Sir Michael Herbert who had been Ambassador in Washington, and grandson of the first Lord Herbert of Lea, the Victorian statesman who gave so much help to Florence Nightingale. At Oxford Sidney and his younger brother Michael were extremely successful, with infinite possibilities. They became two of Duff's dearest friends.

Sidney Herbert

Now, in April 1914, Sibbie was twenty-seven and Sidney twenty-two. He had been accepted as a Conservative candidate for Parliament and all seemed set fair for his future. He was extremely gay and attractive and, although he was in no sense an intellectual, Sibbie fell deeply in love with him, and in a sense remained so for good. Their love affair lasted, with some stresses and strains, throughout the war, and might well have lasted longer if circumstances had been different. Apart from my letters and very few others, his were the only ones she kept, and she left instructions that after her death they were to be burned unread. This was done.

Back in early July 1914 there occurred a tragedy, appalling enough at the time, and in retrospect a foretaste of 'the hell where youth and laughter go' that was to occupy the next four years. Edward Horner and Constantine Benckendorff, son of the Russian Ambassador, gave an evening party in a boat on the Thames. Among the guests were Sibbie, Diana Manners, Iris Tree, Denis Anson, Katharine and Raymond Asquith. A good deal had been drunk when Denis Anson, a strong swimmer, dived off the boat to swim to the shore. He was soon in difficulty, and Benckendorff and a bandsman swam to his rescue. Duff made desperate efforts to follow them, but with his jacket half off Diana and Sibbie managed to pinion and hold him, despite his struggles and curses. Benckendorff just managed to reach the shore, but Anson and the bandsman were drowned. The shock of this calamity stayed with all those present for a long time.

Later in the month our family moved to a rented house at Seaford in Sussex for the summer holidays. From there Sibbie wrote to Iris:

> I got up at five this morning and went out in a boat with Eugenio and Nellie, caught sixteen whiting and a long grey eel, rowed back a bit, took a surprisingly good header into the cold sea, and swam over half a mile to shore, amidst roars of applause from the Capuggis. Otherwise my life here is as regular as a convict's, and every day I wait to hear news that will break my heart.

She had not long to wait, for on 4 August war was declared. To add to her distress I was seriously ill with scarlet fever, which made it impossible to give up the Seaford house immediately. As soon as I was deemed out of quarantine, all my belongings, as was then obligatory, had to be burned, and the tearful placing of my beloved teddy-bear on top of the bonfire is my earliest memory of the Great War.

PART THREE : THE STRESS OF WAR

Last noon beheld them full of lusty life;
Last eve in Beauty's circle proudly gay;
The Midnight brought the signal-sound of strife,
The Morn the marshalling in arms, – the Day
Battle's magnificently-stern array!

BYRON

[1]

THE OUTBREAK of war was so sudden, and by most people so unexpected, that many decisions were taken too quickly and without intelligent foresight. Directly we got back from Seaford the house in Stanhope Street was given up, furniture stored, servants dismissed. My father obtained a commission in the Royal Fusiliers, and for the next five years my mother, Deirdre and I had no home, and often no money, for an officer's pay (my father eventually rose to the rank of Major), even with family allowances, did not cover our most modest expenses, let alone school-fees and doctors' bills.

I cannot easily disentangle the welter of London hotels and other houses in which we stayed during those years, but some are still vividly remembered. Our first refuge was with the old Hart-Davises. My grandfather had recently retired from his post with Lord Ellesmere and had bought a large house in Kent. Although he had never experienced active service he was an old soldier, and now, with the blast of war blowing in his ears, he did his best to imitate the action of the tiger. He played a leading part in the local Territorials, where he was promoted from Captain to Lieutenant-Colonel, and began to draw up plans for the evacuation of his house in the event of enemy invasion. But he never got beyond the first instruction, which was that his mother-in-law, who was in her early nineties, was to be strapped into a dogcart and driven away across Dartford Heath. No destination was ever stipulated, which was not surprising, since she would in fact have been travelling towards the enemy.

My grandfather was genial, friendly and everywhere well liked. Moreover he was talented in various ways. He published books on deer-stalking and angling, at both of which he was adept, as well as a history of Wardley Hall. For private circulation he compiled an immense genealogy, in which he traced his family back to the dark ages, filling in the inevitable gaps with lively imagination. He was a crack billiards-player, a fanatical golfer and unscrupulous in getting what he wanted: he borrowed a large horse-drawn roller from the local golf-club and later sold it to my father. He also drew and painted in water-colour and was an accomplished wood-carver. We loved to watch him meticulously at work with his rounded chisels and little wooden hammer: some of the chairs he made were works of art. He had a fund of tall stories, which he always remembered with advantages, and we used to ask for them again and again, eager to discover how they had been enlarged and improved since their last telling. One of our favourites was his account of how, as a young officer after a heavy night in the mess, he woke so late that he was obliged to shave on horseback on his way to morning parade. Such mundane questions as 'Where did you put the soap, Grandad?' he brushed aside as he and his charger got into their stride. Rich too was the anecdote of his brother who, before our time, had been sent out to South Africa to seek his fortune. He was something of a cricketer, and by the time the story about him reached its apogee Uncle Sid had been summoned at the last minute to play in an important match, had ridden a hundred miles on horseback, swum two large rivers on his horse, scored a century and taken all the wickets, before riding and swimming his way home.

My grandmother had been a keen horsewoman in youth, but was now much reduced by digestive and circulatory ailments. She ate little except Benger's Food and habitually carried about a silver ball filled with hot water to ward off chilblains. Both the old people were kind to us in a conventional way, but they disapproved of many of my mother's words and actions, though they veiled their disapprobation behind a façade of insincere and sentimental euphemisms: anything they deemed unbecoming or original they described as 'quaint'. Years after they were both dead, I came upon some sweets whose name Deirdre and I agreed exactly, if unkindly, described them: Ye Olde Treacle Humbugs.

Living with such conventional in-laws cannot have been easy for my mother, and we all three much preferred our second harbour, where we spent the greater part of the war. This was my beloved Aunt Steffie's rambling old house, Norton Priory, near Selsey in Sussex. Her wealthy husband Arthur Levita (a partner in my father's stockbroking firm) had died in 1910, leaving her with two small daughters, Violet and Enid. Steffie was gay and beautiful, with lovely long dark hair, of which she was justly proud. At the beginning of the war she was very much in love with Tommy Agar-Robartes of the Coldstream Guards. She was always particularly affectionate to me, perhaps because she had wanted a son of her own. Unlike Sibbie she found foreign languages difficult, was furious when in France she heard tiny children talking perfect French, and having no Italian she thought it would be easier for my mother's old maid if she addressed her in broken English: 'Emma, where are ze slippers?' She loved her food and had a superb cook. One day, stopping in the larder for a snack on her way to play tennis, and seeing a chicken plucked and trussed ready for the oven, she gave it a bash with her racket, exclaiming 'Take that, you indecent bird!'

The house was an exciting one for children, with several staircases and long dark passages in which we four played rather frightening games of hide-and-seek. There were said to be ghosts, but we never saw any. In summer the large hall was filled with pots of lilies standing in large wooden cradles, and their scent came up the polished oak staircase and spread through the whole house. Outside there was a large garden, the lawn laid out for golf-croquet, of which a great deal was played. We were fascinated by a medlar tree and its peculiar fruit. We made special friends with Reeves, the odd-job man, who lived in the bothie with the gardeners and was an expert ratcatcher. A short walk along a rough road through water-meadows brought one to the steep, stony beach, where we timorously bathed. Except for a lodge at the entrance to the drive, and a church just outside the gates, there was no building within sight. This delightfully peaceful place, which we called simply The Priory, soon became the nearest we had to a home during the years of war.

But Sibbie was no happier there than in Kent. Richard came down whenever he had leave, until he went for training to Fermoy in Ireland, but otherwise she was alone with Steffie and the children. From the Priory she wrote to Iris:

> Here I am all alone, watching the last leaves fall; a stranger to drink and fashion. Send me a song I can sing to the icy brown waves that beat on this barren shore; a poem that I can murmur to myself at night, when the wind shakes the rafters, and the ghosts, sick with *ennui*, pace the panelled passages . . . I feel that my life is not all it might be. Yesterday I went to the village church and sat by the pillar

alone. Walked eleven miles in the afternoon. The children quarrel, Richard coughs, and Nurse Veda has got indigestion.

Veda Chaffer was our nursery governess for several of these years. I was devoted to her.

In April 1915 Duff began to keep a regular diary and at once recorded that at the Priory he 'had to do some difficult negotiatory work between Sibbie and Richard as regards their future', but with no satisfactory outcome. No wonder that whenever Sidney was on leave from the Royal Horse Guards, Sibbie dashed up to London to be with him. They lunched and dined at the Café Royal, the Eiffel Tower, the Cavendish Hotel, with Iris, Raymond Asquith, Bimbo Tennant, Osbert Sitwell, Ivo Grenfell, Hugo Rumbold, Alan Parsons, Rothesay Stuart-Wortley, Violet Keppel, Elizabeth Asquith and many others. All these friends called her Sybil. Then early in October came the news that Tommy Robartes had been killed in action. Steffie was inconsolable and had to be given morphia. Duff and Sibbie stayed with her.

And so the year dragged on, with alternate periods of rusticity and rather forced jollification. In November, on the eve of Felicity Tree's wedding, Osbert Sitwell gave a huge dinner-party at the Ritz, which included Sibbie, Iris and Nancy Cunard, who was to become a close friend: later in this narrative she will speak in her own voice.

Soon after this Sibbie's sister Mione's house burned down. At first Steffie and Sibbie, with little sisterly charity, felt sure that Mione had set fire to it for the insurance-money, but later gave her the benefit of the doubt. Mione had married soon after Sibbie and now had a son of about my age. She was eccentric in dress and behaviour, uncomfortably rather than amusingly.

On 7 December, driving back from dinner with Gilbert Russell, Sibbie's taxi crashed into the railings in Berkeley Square and her face was cut – but not too badly for her to attend what Duff described as a 'failed party at the Cavendish – Sibbie, Nancy, Marjorie Trefusis, Lady Portarlington and at least a dozen men'. Duff's diary is full of such entries as 'Lunched at Carlton with Eddie Grant, Sidney, Sibbie and Evan Morgan'. And Sibbie saw in the new year at the house of Edwin and Venetia Montagu in Queen Anne's Gate, with Sidney, Bettine Stuart-Wortley, the Raymond Asquiths and Raymond's father the Prime Minister.

To cheer her up at the Priory came two of the very few letters she kept.

Mione and Steffie

One was from the poet Evan Morgan, who later became the second Viscount Tredegar:

Sybil

How too too kind and marvellously understanding of the frailty of human nature you are. No wonder Sidney loves you and appreciates you. A man could, I feel, tell you anything and you would understand. Seldom have I met anyone so kind of heart and anyone who would make so good and trustworthy a friend.

I do hope you will always have the best time, the happiest and most joyous. You deserve it! Iris spoke much of you and now I can understand why. If Fate permits we must, if it doesn't bore you, meet again.

Till then peace and joy and much happiness in all your undertakings. Evan

The other was from Gilbert Russell:

My dear Sybil,

You are the most adorable and interesting and intelligent and lovable and intimate friend I've ever had – funny, but I feel greater friends and less fear of misunderstanding with you than I can remember before, and yet you're *archi-très-femme* and bless you for it.

Gilbert

[3]

1916 was a year of mounting tension. Sibbie fell ill and had to go into a London nursing-home, where she was visited by Patrick Shaw-Stewart and Osbert Sitwell, both home on leave. Then came the agonising time of Sidney's embarkation leave and his departure for France on 14 March. She took to her bed again, overwhelmed with longing and apprehension. When Richard came back on leave she told him of her love for Sidney. This may have eased her conscience a little, but the basic situation was unchanged. Sidney had several times begged her to leave Richard and marry him, but she always refused, knowing that if she did she would inevitably lose possession of her children, the only stabilising influence in the whirlpool of her life, and this sacrifice she simply could not accept. In the lonely misery of later years she often said 'I wish I had married Sidney', but it is at least doubtful whether he would have accepted the responsibility, for he died a bachelor and seemed to prefer love affairs with safely married women. Twice, with a long interval, Sibbie copied out these lines by W. E. Henley:

> There's a regret
> So grinding, so immitigably sad,
> Remorse thereby feels tolerant, even glad . . .
> Do you not know it yet?

[4]

Iris had gone to America with her father, and did not return until after the war. Gradually Nancy took her place in Sibbie's affections. At the Priory on 1 May Sibbie recorded:

A lovely day. Went to lunch with Nancy at Aldwick; brought her back here for tea. Took little Rupert to school; felt very sad when I got back after leaving him. Had a letter from Mike telling me Sidney has been slightly wounded. Felt too worried and anxious: terrible night.

Sidney's wound soon mended, but I was for three terms a weekly boarder, with my cousins Violet and Enid, at a school with a splendidly sibilant address: Seal House, Seal Road, Selsey-on-Sea, Sussex. It was kept by two sisters, the Misses Donkin. I was not actively unhappy there, despite a compulsory cold bath every morning and terrifying riding-lessons, but this first separation from mother, nurse and sister upset me a good deal, and on my first week-end leave, when I found my mother at the Priory, surrounded by a large party which included Lady Randolph Churchill, I rushed into her arms, sobbing uncontrollably.

Duff often came to the Priory at week-ends and recorded

20 May Sibbie met me at Chichester. Staying in the house are only she, Mione, Mother and Tolly Wingfield, who is trying to marry Steffie and will, I believe, succeed. An excellent dinner. Played Slippery Jane afterwards.

21 May A beautiful day. Daylight saving began. In the afternoon Sibbie and I motored over to Bognor. Viola and Alan [Parsons] were staying there with their children. We went first to see them, and then to Craigwell [Aldwick], where was Nancy with all the Churchills. Winston was there, painting hard.

In June, Raymond wrote from the Third Grenadiers in France:

Dearest Syb
. . . I suppose it is true, as you say in your strange rococo dialect, that we have 'drifted apart', but that was inevitable from the moment you set up as Sidney's faithful wife and gave him a first mortgage on your time. After all, the man was never born who could stand being chucked for dinner. In the days when you were still a free-lance it was otherwise. However, even Homer nods and I suppose you must be allowed to be faithful for a little to someone, though I confess I never thought you would carry it to such extreme as you have done.

And Patrick from Salonica:

Darling Sybil,
. . . In your letter you complain of stagnation at Selsey Bill and of the difficulty of finding interest in Things. And then you show at least a gleam of interest by your enquiry on the subject of masochism. [*There follows an analysis of masochism and sadism.*] And yet you suffer from lack of interest in Things. We all do, my dear: and it is of a piece with your little outburst about the War. It is simplicity itself: the War takes from us the People we want, and defies us in that mutilated condition to amuse ourselves with Things. It further complicates the

matter by oppressing us, if we are women, by the fretfulness of inaction and sometimes by acute anxiety: or, if we are men, by varying degrees of discomfort, humiliation, remoteness and danger. In such circumstances is it possible to have an interest in Things? I think it is possible to retain it, but certainly this is a difficult time to cultivate it. I for instance have had since I left Oxford (or more strictly since about a year before) a taste for general reading which has grown with repression: the last of my time at Oxford I was compelled to specialise in every word I read, and since then in times of peace, as you very well know, Baring Bros, tennis, dining, dancing and love have usually taken most of the time between 8 a.m. and 3.30 a.m. and left only too little surplus to bestow on sleep. The war has given me boundless leisure and the delight of enfranchisement is still acute. Lately I have been reading masses, but rather circumscribed by the repertoire of the one bookshop in Salonica – Mignet's *French Revolution*, Holland Rose's *Napoleon, The Bible in Spain, Anna Karenina, The Dark Forest*, Macaulay's *History* (finished), Gilbert Murray's *Rise of the Greek Epic*, some Henry James, and some Lucretius.

If I might suggest, don't make too prodigious an effort about Things just now (though *why not revert to Greek?*) but make some use of such People as are available. That is not a suggestion of disloyalty, but of tension relief. I'm *so* sorry Sidney wasn't more lengthily wounded.

Sibbie now began working as a student-nurse at Greylingwell Hospital, Chichester, and studying for the two certificates she needed before she could be given more responsible work. But in the middle of August Steffie disappeared with Tolly Wingfield, after telling all the servants at the Priory to take a holiday. Homeless again, we stayed first at the Regent Palace Hotel, and Sibbie started befriending, perhaps more out of pity than affection, a young man called Gray Edwards. One evening he called at the hotel, saying he had no money and nowhere to sleep. We were all three sleeping in one room, and my mother told him that for this night he could sleep on the floor. He did so, was found there by a chambermaid in the morning, reported to the management, and we were all turned out of the hotel. Ford's Hotel in Manchester Street was our next refuge, as often in the next two years, during which we also stayed in the Felix and Cavendish Hotels in Jermyn Street and the Welbeck Palace and Clifton Hotels in Welbeck Street.

Now the Battle of the Somme, which had been raging since 1 July, began to affect Sibbie. Raymond Asquith was killed there on 15

September, Bimbo Tennant a week later. Her fears for Sidney grew daily. A telegram in those days was a dreadful object, but on 5 October Sibbie received one to say Sidney was home on leave. She hurried to London to spend it with him. Five days later Steffie was married to Tolly Wingfield, and on the morrow Duff 'dined at Carlton Grill with Nancy, Sydney Fairbairn, Sibbie, Sidney and Diana. A jolly dinner – three magnums'.

But with Sidney's return to France jollity gave way to fearful apprehension, desperation and despair. On 1 November Duff noted: 'Under the purifying influence of Alex Thynne, Sibbie has sworn to give up smoking and drinking absolutely for a year and has already done so for two or three days.' This resolution was short-lived, but the rest of the year was comparatively peaceful. On Christmas Day Lady Agnes recorded 'a very cheerful lunch at Steffie's flat [in Berkeley House, Hay Hill] – all my four children and five grandchildren'. To which Duff added: 'an excellent lunch – perfect turkey and champagne. It was all very *en famille* and correct. I enjoyed it'. On Boxing Day we all had high tea in Steffie's flat and went to the first night of the Drury Lane pantomime. There was a dense fog, and somehow we all piled into one taxi.

[5]

1917 began with a flurry of nursing activity. Sibbie attended Lady Falkland's classes in London, taking copious notes, and at the end of February was awarded certificates of proficiency in First Aid and Home Nursing by the St John Ambulance Association. She cheerfully bought three blue overalls, six aprons, six pairs of sleeves, and four caps, for a total of £2.4.1, and returned to Greylingwell whenever she was not in London or busy with the children. Patrick Shaw-Stewart was on leave in London, and Sibbie recorded these bets between him, Duff and Katharine Asquith:

49 Bedford Square, W.C.

Duff bets Katharine 15 to 1 in ten pounds that Lord Curzon will not be the next Prime Minister

Katharine bets Duff £150 to 10 that Bonar Law will not be the next P.M.

Duff bets Patrick £1500 to 100 that W. S. Churchill will never be P.M.

Patrick bets Duff an even £25 that Lloyd George is Prime Minister of England the day hostilities cease between England and Germany.

Duff bets Patrick £110 to £40 that peace between Great Britain and Germany is not signed in 1917.

[*signed*]   Patrick Shaw-Stewart
Duff Cooper
K.A.

23 February 1917

At the beginning of April Deirdre had to have an operation for a double hernia. My mother and I stayed at Ford's Hotel while she was in a nursing home in Manchester Street. All went well, and at the end of the month my mother took me to begin my four preparatory-school years at Stanmore Park in Middlesex, a long low white house, built by John Vardy in the 1760s for Andrew Drummond, founder of Drummond's Bank. It overlooked wide playing fields that sloped down to a small lake, in which a few aged pike nosed their way around. Once a year the headmaster, Vernon Royle, who had been an England cricketer but was now restricted to a wheel-chair, would fire from the hip at these monstrous fish, but in my time no hits were recorded.

At first all the boys looked enormous and exactly the same, but gradually I sorted them out. Names like Casdagali and Sevastopoulo were surprising, but their destination, like that of almost all the other boys, was nearby Harrow, where no doubt such names were commonplace. The masters were all too old or too unfit for military service. We were taught copperplate handwriting by a gentle bearded old man called Mr Adamsez, and among the phrases we had to copy out for him was a valuable couplet:

> Work hard play hard. Xenophon was a Greek.
> Use your toothbrush daily. Hack no furniture.

By this time there were serious shortages, and the food was appalling. My letters are full of requests for cake and jam. Twice a week for breakfast we were faced by a tepid orange-coloured mess of curried lentils: Mr Bultitude didn't know how lucky he was to get those two sardines.

This more prolonged parting from my mother showed us both how necessary we were to each other. I had always believed her capable of working what seemed to be miracles, and I knew that if I told her the school was unbearable she would somehow contrive to take me away from it. But I realised that I must endure if I could, and after some bad homesickness I settled down, found the school tolerable, and by the end positively enjoyable. During the nine years of my schooling I wrote and posted some sort of a letter to my mother on every day of every term, and she somehow managed to send a daily letter to me. She early taught me always to date my letters, and surprisingly almost always dated hers. Both lots of these letters have survived: they are full of love and longing to be together again, full too of pet-names and long-forgotten family jokes. Mine are banal, for schoolboys have little news or time, but hers describe her doings and her friends. They are all love-letters, and when I have quoted from them and finished this record I shall destroy them, for they can mean little to anyone else. She enjoyed writing letters, using a relief nib and a bottle of ink, of which she liked the smell. She always addressed the envelope first (as I still do) but did not always fill it. After her death dozens of addressed envelopes were found in her writing-table drawer.

I made one lifelong friend at Stanmore, a slim, shy, friendly boy called Wyndham Cremer. Later he became Ketton-Cremer, grew stouter and looked more and more like an eighteenth-century squire who had mislaid his wig. He wrote lives of Gray and Horace Walpole, several volumes of Norfolk history, and a fine account of his lovely Norfolk home, Felbrigg, near Cromer, where I happily visited him at intervals over the next fifty years. He was a faithful and affectionate friend.

[6]

In August Sidney came home on leave and Sibbie stayed with him at the Berkeley. Duff, released from the Foreign Office, and training for the army at Bushey, came up and lunched with them. It was now that the roystering figure of Augustus John appeared in Sibbie's life. Like all the others he was fascinated by her, admired and, after his fashion, loved her. He drew a number of pencil heads of her. She thought him a genius, and during the next year they saw a good deal of each other. But his influence on her was not beneficial: she never had a strong head for liquor, and the minimum that anyone was obliged to drink in John's company was often too much for her. (At that time everyone called him

Sibbie by Augustus John

John: I never heard him called Augustus till many years later.) She needed a stabilising presence, and his was a destructive one. Funnily enough the two people who most often advised her to give up alcohol altogether were John and her brother Duff, two of the most persistent drinkers of their time.

Iris wrote from Havana: 'Tell me about your social status in England now – good or bad form? Pariah or niece of the Duchess of Fife? Marie Beerbohm's companion or Lady Herbert's?' Difficult questions to answer, but perhaps Sibbie was grasping a partial solution when she copied out this passage from Henry James's *Roderick Hudson*: 'My own impression is, that like the most interesting people always, she is a

Sibbie by Augustus John

mixture of better and worse, of good passions and bad, always of passions however: and that whatever she is she is neither stupid nor mean and possibly by a miracle not even false.'

And still the bell tolled for the friends of her youth: on 21 November Edward Horner was killed in France. Only Patrick and Sidney were left now.

On 23 November, taking eight-year-old Deirdre with her, Sibbie went to have a drink with John, who had with him the poet and critic of the 1890s, Arthur Symons, long since released from a mental home, but a dim shadow of his younger self. He was so impressed by the sight of this beautiful little girl (who was probably just bored and hungry) that he wrote this poem about her:

DEIRDRE

There was much crying in the wind
Late last night
As of the crying of a soul that had sinned
And longed for the light.

But I have seen to-day
With John in a café a child
Who seemed so tragic, that play
Was lost to her, never she smiled.

Adorable, passionate,
Loveless, the child in her chair,
Casting her eyes down, sat –
The Sun might have envied her hair.

She had taken my hand, then turned
Her eyes on me, pure as the sky.
If ever a man's heart to her yearned,
Mine did, I know not why.

Café Royal, November 27, 1917

Soon after this John introduced Sibbie to the painter and writer Percy Wyndham Lewis (always called simply Lewis). He had come back from France on compassionate leave because his mother was ill, and soon went back as an official War Artist (John was another). He was dark and handsome, moustached and somewhat gipsy-like in appearance. Sibbie, her heart as always too soon made glad, fell in love with him and he with her. When his first novel *Tarr* came out in 1918 she bought several dozen copies and gave them away to likely supporters, but when Lewis published his autobiography *Blasting and Bombardiering* in 1937 all he could find to say of her was 'She was a woman with a great taste for learning. Her proficiency in Greek was such as to dumbfound Lord Oxford, who was doubtless unaccustomed to hear Greek from the mouths of the aristocratic Amazons of England.' Lewis was always very nice to me, gave me cigarette-cards, which I eagerly collected, and a large two-volume stamp-album.

In the middle of December, towards the end of my second term at Stanmore, I contracted a heavy cold, and the authorities, unwilling to send me home in such a condition, moved me into the school

Wyndham Lewis

sanatorium. Here there was so little supervision and so much room for manoeuvre that we all larked about instead of staying in bed, and my cold became double pneumonia, which in those days was almost a death-warrant. The news reached my mother late at night when she was dining in London with Lewis. In great distress she immediately set out for Stanmore, by the last train and then by means of a long walk through icy darkness, the faithful Lewis at her side. They found me in an oxygen tent at the crisis of my illness, but my mother's presence tipped the scale, and in a few days I was pronounced out of danger. When my Aunt Steffie heard this news she exclaimed, 'What, all that worry for nothing!'

I was just well enough to be moved before Christmas, which my mother and I spent alone together in Augustus John's studio-house in Mallord Street, Chelsea, where Duff visited us. To celebrate the new year, and my recovery, my mother gave a small party there. Neighbours complained of the noise, and John pretended to be angry, though heaven knows the party was mild in comparison with some of his.

Unknown then, the bell had tolled once more, for on 30 December Patrick Shaw-Stewart, the last of Sibbie's classical friends, had been killed. He had originally joined the Hood Battalion of the Royal Naval Division, and on their way to the Dardanelles had commanded the firing party at the burial of Rupert Brooke on the island of Scyros. He survived the whole of the Allied occupation of the Gallipoli peninsula, and then served for a year at or near Salonica. Finding this too tame, he wangled his way back to the Hood Battalion in France and was killed there commanding the battalion. He was twenty-nine. On a blank page of his copy of Housman's *Shropshire Lad*, written in his hand, was this fine poem. It is a fitting epitaph:

I saw a man this morning
  Who did not wish to die:
I ask, and cannot answer,
  If otherwise wish I.

Fair broke the day this morning
  Against the Dardanelles;
The breeze blew soft, the morn's cheeks
  Were cold as cold sea-shells.

But other shells are waiting
  Across the Ægean sea,
Shrapnel and high explosive,
  Shells and hells for me.

O hell of ships and cities,
  Hell of men like me,
Fatal second Helen,
  Why must I follow thee?

Achilles came to Troyland
  And I to Chersonese:
He turned from wrath to battle
  And I from three days' peace.

Was it so hard, Achilles,
  So very hard to die?
Thou knowest and I know not —
  So much the happier I.

I will go back this morning
  From Imbros over the sea;
Stand in the trench, Achilles,
  Flame-capped, and shout for me.

[7]

At the beginning of 1918 I was still recuperating, and did not go back to Stanmore until the summer term. Instead I stayed happily at the Priory with my mother and Deirdre. My father was on a Staff course at Cambridge. Augustus John strongly recommended his eccentric friend John Hope-Johnstone as a holiday-tutor. He came to the Priory, but when we assembled for lessons he was usually playing the flute in another room. He challenged all comers to box with him, and the milkman, who was a much better performer, repeatedly knocked him down, saying 'Sorry, sir' each time.

Exercise was thought good for us, and, accompanied by my mother or Veda, we often trudged along the road to Selsey, lured on by promise of a bar of chocolate or an ice-cream at what was locally known as the Mikadoo Cayf. The distance was only a mile or two, but to us it seemed endless.

Two notable eccentrics lived in Selsey at this time. One was Sir Archibald Hamilton, fifth and third Baronet. His house was almost on the beach, with incongruous and lamenting peacocks in the windswept garden. Indoors there was so much furniture that one had to edge round it. He usually gave us fish for lunch and astonished me by covering it with mustard. His remarks to my mother always began 'Prithee, Gracious Lady', and all his conversation was couched in a fantasticated eighteenth-century style: he was the first person I heard describe St John's Wood as The Shady Groves of the Evangelist. Many years ago he had become a Mahommedan, but he had now declined upon the Presidency of the Selsey Unionist Society. Although he was twice married, I remember him as permanently alone in his overcrowded house, with the sea and the peacocks in noisy competition outside.

The other eccentric was Edward Heron-Allen, who lived in a much bigger house in the middle of the little town. He was an amateur polymath of genius: in *Who's Who* he gave his recreations as 'Persian Literature; Marine Zoology; Meteorology; Heraldry; Bibliography; Occasional Essays and Scientific Romances; Auricula and Asparagus Culture'. He had been a friend of Oscar Wilde, who developed or appropriated some of his ideas. Originally a solicitor, he had published books on violin-making, cheirosophy and local history, as well as novels, volumes of verse, and a literal translation of Omar Khayyam. He was made a Fellow of the Royal Society for his work on minute marine organisms called Foraminifera. All this was unknown to me as I played with his two daughters in their large garden, while he, in somewhat dandified dress of an earlier time, searched on the shingly beach for the origins of life. I fell deeply in love with his younger daughter Armorel, a dark-haired child of great liveliness, charm and beauty. I never saw her after the war, and she was killed in a car-crash when she was an undergraduate. I was much moved when an Oxford friend of hers told me that Armorel had several times spoken of me.

Armorel Heron-Allen

[8]

But Sibbie had had enough of staying in other people's houses, however friendly and hospitable. 'I *do* wish,' she wrote, 'we had got a house of our own, oh *so* much. It makes everything difficult having to consider so many people.' She toyed with the idea of trying to buy her sister Mione's house in Notting Hill Gate, but money was lacking, and she was forced to abandon her hopes until in the summer she gained some temporary independence. Meanwhile Sidney was again on leave and she with him, going to the new edition of *The Bing Boys* and seeing a lot of Duff and their other friends. 'Went back to the Montagus' with Sibbie and Sidney,' wrote Duff, 'where we drank champagne and ate caviare.' Sidney seemed more than ever precious as, one by one, his contemporaries were mown down.

The next party was at the end of April – a farewell one for Duff, whom Sibbie, Diana and others sadly saw off to the war, from which he triumphantly returned in October, unscathed and with a D.S.O. My grandmother was grievously upset by his departure, and to be near and comfort her we three stayed for a time at the Welbeck Palace Hotel. From there, after taking me back to school early in May, my mother wrote: 'I am very tired of this hotel. Will send cricket bat.' During this term I caught chicken-pox, and for the next few years was seldom free for long from some illness or other. In Gibbon's words, 'of the various and frequent disorders of my childhood my own recollection is dark: nor do I wish to expatiate on so disgusting a topic', but the delightful sequel was usually a week or two at Brighton. We must have stayed at every hotel on the front from the Royal York to the Princes in Hove, and never since have I arrived at Brighton Station without experiencing again the twin pleasures of truancy and returning health.

One day during the summer term Augustus John drove my mother and Deirdre to Stanmore and took me out for the day. We picnicked beside a quiet lane and, lying on his back, John drew little sketches of Deirdre and me.

Otherwise my mother was at the Priory from May to July, and saw something of Nancy at nearby Aldwick. And now Nancy shall speak for herself. It is seldom a good plan to interpolate other people's writing in a straight narrative: their style may well show up the inadequacy of the narrator's; it may interrupt the flow, and so on. But Nancy's memories seem to me so well written, so self-revealing, and so totally in accord with all I remember of the scenes she describes, that they can only add to the portrait I am trying to draw. Moreover her words come from, as it were, an outsider and must therefore carry additional weight. However hard I strive for strict objectivity, I realise that I must always be, consciously or subconsciously, prejudiced. I have omitted a small part of what Nancy wrote, mainly rhetorical questions and forgotten jokes – nothing relevant or important. I should perhaps point out that in age she was exactly half-way between my mother and me. In the summer of 1918, with which Nancy largely deals, she was twenty-two, my mother thirty-one, and I eleven.

Rupert and Deirdre by Augustus John

INTERLUDE : 'MY LIBERATOR'

(Sybil remembered for Rupert and Deirdre by Nancy)

ASSUREDLY I must have heard about Sybil some time before I first met her in 1913, and then met her only passingly with many others during the last season in Venice before the war. I was seventeen, on the edge only of that society of brilliant or striking English personalities who all knew each other so well. Of Sybil it was said that she was 'a very clever woman indeed'. Then twenty-seven years old, it was immediately perceptible that she was also very much *en vogue*. Her prestige came, in part, from her knowledge of Greek and from her capacity in discussing the classics, books and ideas with scholarly men. Her looks, her charm, and her unexpectedness were other assets.

The impact was immediate; exciting my imagination, she seemed mysterious in I know not what romantic way. Was it the first time I saw her that she wore that remarkable dress? A straight, full-length, close-fitting creation in white chiffon with large black zebra stripes, it had long sleeves and was cut very low back and front. And surely she was the first woman to have short hair? Admirably bobbed or shingled, a honey-coloured, assertive glory, it swung free or lay in neat undulations on a well-proportioned head. How well it suited her face; to me that face belonged to a very ancient century, coming from some remote northern Atlantic island. Her appearance pleased me enormously: the expressiveness of her blue eyes, slightly tip-tilted nose, and thin, straight mouth. What I felt at seeing her could well go into words heard twenty years later from a French workman, spoken half in astonishment and half in admiration: '*Ça, c'est quelqu'un!*' Yes, exactly that.

She was very much surrounded at all these Venetian dinners, dances and Lido-hours, and I remember well Raymond Asquith's adulation and the great approval of the then P.M. – Henry Asquith. In a background of tuberoses in great vases near the open windows of those hot September nights in the *palazzi*, a stefanotis. That, as I heard him do, was what the P.M. called her: Stefanotis. It is a rare flower, its bloom a

Nancy Cunard by Curtis Moffat

little waxen, as precious as a gardenia, as a camellia – an exotic whiteness.

I must have seen her next in the spring of 1914 in London and, as the last summer season before the war progressed, I would find her at all the parties given by the 'Coterie' (its centre and animator Diana), where one enjoyed oneself entirely, very much more than at the formal receptions and functions. Our own evenings would be at Viola Parsons's, at Raymond and Katharine's and at a few others. At that time she was Iris's great friend and we hardly knew each other. Then came the war with its great changes overnight. The Coterie would meet at Kettner's a good deal, at those dinners so quickly arranged for the young men coming up from camp not so very long before they went out to the front, and Sybil was at most of these.

The first half of 1915 was lavish in parties, particularly those at 94 Lancaster Gate, which George G. Moore, the American millionaire, businessman (and even 'mystery-man') had taken and where Lord

French lived when not in France. I would sometimes have the arranging of them: 'I want a dinner of twelve, and thirty or forty people afterwards – for *tonight*. Can you do it?' Moore would phone. I see Sybil here in a most beautiful dress of pure gold. She is in a ravishing black chiffon one at other parties in the Cavendish, arranged impromptu for those going to France and Flanders or come suddenly on leave. Our spirits were high in those days, kept going by the excitement of war, the courage of those returning from it who never had a word to say about its horrors. Sybil was always at such evenings; it seems to me she would arrive rather late and her entrée would cause a stir. More often than a dance it would be 'just a party in the Elinor' – Mrs Lewis's abbreviation for the Elinor Glyn Room, so-named, I suppose, on account of its impressive purple couch. After much champagne the cry would go up for 'stunts', and on the spot Duff, Sidney Herbert, Hugo Rumbold and Evelyn Beerbohm would don the character of French, British, German, Nicaraguan and other ambassadors at cross-purposes with each other in several languages. What might be termed 'Scientists in Conclave' (same style, same brilliant improvisation) would follow – the evening rounded off, very late, with choruses from all present, of songs like 'The Twelve Days of Christmas' and 'I'll drink out of the Pint, my boy.'

I cannot think now how we had such high spirits. Everything – war-work, week-ends, parties, seemed to go with such speed. The very word (in another context) recalls a quip, verbatim. It is Sybil getting into a taxi at the Berkeley, saying 'Drive *like hell* to the Ritz [which was exactly opposite]!' The driver appreciated the address so much that never a more beautiful *demi-tour* can have been executed in any street in the world.

Sybil in the Eiffel Tower Restaurant, with Iris, Guevara, Gertler, Augustus John, Wyndham Lewis, in the Café Royal Brasserie, in – of course, in 'Fitz', that slightly sinister-looking studio at 8 Fitzroy Street which Iris furnished so well on nothing but a few contributions from some of us. No matter how it looked to a newcomer, it soon acquired atmosphere. There was a lino floor of large black-and-white squares, a gas-fire and an ancient gas-light by it, a large black velvet sofa, scarlet panels around two beautiful old bow-windows, a table at which poems were written, sometimes a few bottles and a pack of cards. Surely it was here that Epstein made his fine head of Iris in 1915? 'Fitz' was of very great use. Here one could fill in the hiatus between dinner and a party, play cards, talk to one's love, get warm after the icy streets of winter.

If I could recall just when Iris went to America, I could say when Sybil and I became very great friends. Iris bequeathed us to each other, tacitly. And yet I think she told each to see as much of the other as possible. Till then I knew almost nothing of Sybil's life, Richard being rather in the background – perhaps at the war by then. Iris and I had been very much together, but probably she had seen even more of Sybil. The gap made by her departure was great; Sybil's friendship and companionship with me date from that moment.

Till now what had impressed me most about her was all that *panache*, and style, and 'riding high'. Very soon now I discovered the courage and spirit and all the sterling quality of her as well. Those quickly-changing moods, indeed at moments the *volte-face* (sometimes explained later, and sometimes never) did not perplex me long. Oh what a tease she could be! And ironical. And then full of good-will and helpful; taking so much trouble for those who had her interest, she was most generous always. A very complex character. The realisation of this came much more fully, of course, when we shared Bagpuize. One was always in love in those days, and it might often be with two or three men at the same time. Sybil and I were alike in this, and there were many probing conversations into the subject. Above all – yes, what, above all? Without going into psychological depths, above all this: the style of her, the cut and dash in general, and in all sorts of small, physical details. I remember my admiration at the way she once lit a cigarette from an electric heater.

1917 – I was now twenty-one and married, Sybil being ten years older than me, and how ridiculous it seemed that Her Ladyship [Nancy's mother] and Richard (separately) should complain that we had a bad influence on each other! Sydney Fairbairn enjoyed Sybil's liveliness and gaiety when she came to our house during that abominable period of my life – marriage – but was slightly uneasy, it being obvious that she and I lived in a very different rhythm to his and that of the bridge-playing guardsmen. I did not see her frequently now (once it had been daily), and the occasion on which she arrived in mid-afternoon at Montagu Square with a request for an immediate bath comes back to me like an apparition. After the brief vision of Sybil in the bath, with her neat little *toque* on, gay and laughing, she was gone again. Memory failing one unaccountably at times, this is the only picture it yields me of Sybil in all 1917. She came to play bridge and poker, came to parties in that house when Bruce Ottley would spend the night at the piano – marvellously so – between two bottles of champagne, but where is the detail to it all?

The beginning of a belief in the eventual end of my bitter and preposterous married life came while reading *South Wind* as soon as it appeared in the summer of that year. This sounds affected, *précieux* and without any logical connexion, and I cannot explain it, yet there it was: this existence would not go on for ever – I kept on feeling this amid the pages of the adorable book. There must have been many more dreary bridge foursomes, some of them with Sybil, before, somehow in the spring of 1918, I discovered Oxford. Oxford was embodied in 29 Holywell – the house, I think, of a don called Dr Carlyle, now let to Ralph Grimthorpe and Rothesay Stuart-Wortley and two other 'chaps', all of them in the Air Force. I have a photograph of Sybil taken the day she came from Selsey to see me at Craigweil near Bognor about then. There is a conservatory at the back of my mind here – I mean, it was in the conservatory that she and I talked so long that day about life and being in love, and how to get through long, boring periods when everything seems to stand still. That summer we explored Holywell together, where there was always gaiety and drink, even riotous singing of an evening with the 'chaps' – undergraduate songs, no doubt, with new words to some of them, such as 'Dr Carlyle jumped right over Mrs Carlyle's back'; Ralph, Rothesay and Sybil being very proficient at this.

Now Sybil and I decided on finding a house together in the country, and Sydney left for the front. But who was it who discovered Bagpuize? I think this was accomplished, via a house-agent, rather hastily by me. Hastily and 'sketchily', because, when I had seen it, I could not but tell Sybil that some people might consider it to be rather depleted of furniture; inconvenient of access; excessive in rental; and even tarnished by some kind of odd reputation (we never found out on what score). We took it on the spot for four months.

There was one last hilarious evening in London at the Queen's Restaurant in Sloane Square: Sybil and Augustus John, Guevara and myself, and maybe one or two others. We sat late and drank long and, as so often when Sybil was present, everything went with a swing, she being a brilliant talker in most moods. John too was very happy and this manifested itself in a regular spate of drawings by him all over the tablecloth – which we immediately bought – to the perplexity of the waiters who clustered round admonishing him for spoiling their napery.

And then the day came, early in August 1918, when the four of us, you and Deirdre, Sybil and myself, and also my *soubrettish* French maid Palmyre and good British Mrs Kerwood, the cook, made the move to Bagpuize. Was its real name The New House, Kingston Bagpuize?

Whatever it was called, it remained Bagpuize to us, the name being such a pleasure to say, and to read.

A magnificent day it was, full of sun and high wind, great white clouds moving across the sky and everyone in a fine temper as we arrived laden with household utensils in the middle of the afternoon. Immediately you and I and Deirdre were running through the garden, inspecting everything in the house. It enchanted us, for it had so much character. Do you remember the place? Built, I should say, in the early part of last century, it had no outstanding architectural features but atmosphere a-plenty. Surrounded by flat fields, it stood at the end of a narrow road with an immense avenue of lordly old beech-trees running parallel on the right, across a stretch of grass. Roses and flowers we found in the somewhat abandoned garden, but devil a gardener; I remember no one ever working outside the whole time we were there.

Sure enough, the house was rather bare, very un-English in its proportions and style, and we were immediately installed. Some eleven miles from Oxford (no doubt the proximity of Holywell greatly influenced our taking it) Ralph and Rothesay would often come over, as did Alexander, the third of their group, known as 'A' – the strong silent man who had spent years in Rangoon, knew about machines, was modest in conversation to the point of silence until the fifth glass or so, and who had – oddly, I thought – taken to me.

As the first days went by, I discovered something new: that I could get on wonderfully with you and Deirdre – eleven and nine years old – as if never the faintest shyness had existed in me on the score of children. Until then, *gêne* or boredom with children had been the case. Now why was this, do you suppose? Even with all your niceness, good manners, charm and lack of timidity, I was rather surprised at myself. I think it must have been because of the way Sybil had been with you from your earliest years, the way she always treated you, not as an admonishing parent, but on an equal footing. My own childhood was filled with the disproportions created by 'grown-ups', a relic of Victorianism, when children had to be 'talked down to' (to say the least). When adult, I never liked being with any child, until I knew you and Deirdre.

The next discovery was about Sybil's character and the progressive effect she had on me. What was going to happen when the war was over – how should I know the way to put an end to this awful marriage of mine? Sybil has been a very important element in my life. She was a great influence then, at an acutely critical time. Let it be said that she *liberated* me from the oppression I had been living in for nearly two years.

Through her I seemed now to realise that, although one can half-live for someone else, forcing oneself to this despite a great unwillingness, the time comes when everything in one clamours 'Enough!' Not consciously on her part, she liberated me, brought me back the personality I had before I was married, and, even more, gave or stimulated in me something new. Soon enough an event came to back this up.

And how, meanwhile, was she? Unhappy with Richard as a husband; the weight of this was heavy on her even while he was in France. She should not (I think) have been married at all. She was an artist. I say this because time and again she would voice ideas, imagining situations and circumstances that belonged to the mind of a creative writer. Her interest in people was very quick and sometimes peculiar, and this she expressed very well indeed in talk. Her letters were enchanting to read. Of constant wonder to me were her character and personality, her independence of mind, now and and again as impulsive as an arrow from the bow, her enthusiasm, the dynamic mood that would suddenly seize her, the introspective one it would pass into. Paradoxical and contradictory were some of her days, when she might seem *exaltée* – a law unto herself, or else something of a mystic. Remember, we were never out of the clutch of war, that is to say, of fear that one or more of those we loved or dearly liked might be killed at any moment.

Happily running about the place and always occupied were you and Deirdre, and it seemed not to impress *you* at all, Rupert, that you were already so very good at school. To us it was obvious you were not only clever, but already manly and independent. Deirdre I saw as rather a dreamy child, self-contained and fond of reading; she would look very lovely among the flowers or engrossed in her book, and then be suddenly very practical and attentive to her rabbits.

We read a good deal, Sybil and I, much of Swinburne's and Meredith's poetry and all the tales of Maupassant, and *A Story-Teller's Holiday* by George Moore, which had just come out. These things are bound up with Bagpuize, as is, even more, Havelock Ellis's *Psychology of Sex*, gaily referred to as 'the six brown books'. Sybil read aloud beautifully and without tiring; her memory for poetry was very good indeed and many were the literary conversations with some of those who came to visit us, such as Ribblesdale and Hutchinson. She was an admirable hostess, and in this house in the fields, that had no recognised distractions of any kind, there was never an empty moment. Copious readings or brief extracts from 'the six brown books' were frequent all

that hot, lovely August and September. After giving Deirdre her lessons
(you had gone back to school by then) Sybil might spend hours writing
letters; they would be full of thoughts and conversations across distance.
Her concentration was then complete while her pen or pencil flew. (Alas
that not one of her letters to me should have escaped the *next* war.)

From Holywell they would come sometimes to fetch us for dinner
unexpectedly – which recalls Sybil as a sort of 'quick-change artist'. Two
minutes ago she would have been in a jersey and trousers, and now – oh
the swing of that skirt, the perfect cut of the tailored jacket over the pale
chemisier, the neat black shoes and white stockings, the whole ensemble
that caused some people at that time to murmur 'rather masculine'!
This is the visual picture I have most of Sybil: the impeccable tailoring,
the set of her head, the straight look in her eyes, along with that quick
and so individual way she had of speaking – a long phrase, as like as not,
with some zestful bit of fantasy at the end of it.

In September or early October Augustus John came down for the
week-end bringing with him an 'unknown quantity' (who drank even
more than anyone else) with bright carmine cheeks and stark black hair,
no hulking young giant from the far-North but a speechless, furtive,
wiry denizen-of-the-desert, found by John I don't know where and
almost without English: the Icelander. A drinking-companion
perhaps? He had written a play in his own tongue, and I think that is all
we learned of him.

About then a new war-directive had been issued: 'Burn less coal!' and
the delight was great when Sybil pointed out that it said, in part, that
people *ought to live together a great deal more*, so as to save heating. This
would hardly have been in our minds after Mrs Kerwood's excellent
'make-do' dinner (as she often called the meals she said she was ashamed
to set before us, 'but the war you know . . .'), accompanied by our nice
red Bordeaux (we even had champagne on occasion, which I would buy
for six shillings and eightpence a bottle), yet we were in rather a huddle
round the fireplace, five or six of us, and the Icelander not in the picture
at all at the moment. Where was he? Suddenly John's great voice
boomed out:

'HJALMAR!'

certain preparatory gestures in a corner being recognizable. With
lumbering swiftness John then arose, took the Icelander by the
shoulders and bundled him into the garden. Imperfectly house-trained!

You have the snapshots of Augustus in uniform with Sybil in a great breeze; of Sybil *à la* cricketer in trousers, cap and blazer; of Sybil and Mione and the Icelander in dressing-gowns, all equally wind-swept. (Really, the days of breezes, winds and even gales at Bagpuize were numerous; it was then those great beeches looked finest of all.)

Kingston Bagpuize: Augustus John and Sibbie

Kingston Bagpuize: Sibbie

Kingston Bagpuize: Mione, Sibbie and the Icelander

With an armful of books, mainly of poetry, Sybil would often go to the garden, and one day she took Augustus, as well as one or two of 'the six brown books', to a haystack, atop of which – the wind having presumably gone down – Augustus fell asleep lengthily and, on being called by her later, leapt from it so fast that he grievously put out his knee. He was a major in the Army at that time, a war-artist. There was already about him that patriarchal grandeur, that suggestion of a solitary prophet, along with the ageless eagle-gaze that I am sure he yet has. I was rather shy of him then, but Sybil humanized all of this aura. (*You* will know how much Augustus appreciated, honoured and loved Sybil.)

Another great artist likewise, although it was a little earlier that Wyndham Lewis so much occupied her mind. She loved him a good deal, and as for Lewis – years later, when I began to know him consecutively in Venice in 1922, he would talk to me about her every day. There was no one like her, he said. Unique as she was, in some respects she had the brain of a man; she understood and could discuss so many things, whereas . . . platters of abuse would be served up about 'despicable little Jewesses', 'scheming little bitches', etc, all of whom had once held his fancy. I listened to much praise of Sybil – a most unusual thing to hear from Lewis. He told me he had been very much in love with her indeed. And, though it was a reciprocal, if difficult and broken-up love, Sybil, while talking to me about him earlier that year, showed me how much she had thought about his character; she went through her own feelings too, and her doubts about him, her longing to see him more often. At Selsey it would have been thought odd if she had written him every day, as she wanted to do, so 'sometimes I wrote twenty letters or so a day just so as to put one in for him without that seeming to mean anything in particular'. She really went over Lewis, bit by bit, and not all of it was without mockery. What did I think of his looks? Having seen Lewis, when I hardly knew him, at his most conspiratorial, alarmingly umbrageous in style and manner, rather a 'tough' in his turned-up collar and pulled-down hat – no, even so I cannot think what prompted me to say that I thought he *looked* like 'a bicycling plumber'. Loud was the laughter.

Who else came to Bagpuize? You were there when Ribblesdale spent a week-end, for there is a snapshot of several people on the grass in front of the house: Cousin Victor and Ralph Grimthorpe and Henry Mond are in it, as well as you and the darling old Lord. You were there too when Peter Broughton-Adderley came on leave, and since then I have told you how intensely in love we were and had been, secretly, for many months, although we had only known each other for five days before he went to the war that previous winter. Mond, who was a friend of Marie Beerbohm's, came three or four times all the way from York, with a chicken and a bottle of chartreuse, and the regularity of his rather maddening company threatened to become such that I sent an involved telegram which caused those visits to cease.

There was also that Saturday to Monday with St John Hutchinson and Mond when Richard somehow irrupted into the week-end, on leave. Things moved steadily from sultry to thunderous, although no-one but myself realised the situation. But what situation? Nothing new had happened to create one. There was always 'a situation' in those times between Sybil and Richard. Alexander had come over from Oxford and it may have been 'A' who encouraged Mond to make such extra strong cocktails that soon everyone was heartily lit and remained so well into the night. When Alexander and I were together a sort of game of 'confidences' would develop, and we must have been at it, sprawled as usual in front of the fireplace, Mond and Hutchie having disappeared somewhere, when a scream rang out from above: Sybil and Richard at the climax of some argument. And now the maids were running about, calling from the stairs. As I hurried towards it all, ready to make a distracting scene with Richard myself, Mond and Hutchie emerged from the sitting-room, ecstatic. Was it really metaphysics that Mond was still discussing? From Hutchie came a babble of delight: he didn't, no he *really* didn't quite know where he was – he kept on telling me – a most delightful feeling, and oh, why not join them? How they impeded me in their alcoholic nirvana! It was very tense upstairs and threatening, and pretty soon Sybil was hurrying down with an arm round Deirdre, who had been awakened and quickly dressed, ready to leave the house forthwith and 'for ever'. I forget just how everything was calmed back to 'sultry'. Mond and Hutchie went on babbling, unaware of Sybil's tense face and the hysterics of the French maid. 'A', prudent and tactful, was 'standing by' ready to intervene if masculine violence should ensue. Richard must have disappeared into his room.

(A local note here: Whatever the doings or goings-on at Bagpuize week-ends, the case of empty bottles and the laundry-basket were never once forgotten but slung on to the Monday morning taxi for Oxford. A sort of decorum seemed to reside in not forgetting essentials.)

There was also the day when George Moore was coming and I had been imagining what a revelation Sybil would be to him and the many, very many questions he would no doubt put to her. Would he go so far as to say in that rolling voice, with that expectant look of his: 'Tell me about your lovers!' as he so often did to me? That would depend on whether they liked each other or no. But now, through nobody's fault, this projected visit coincided with Richard's sudden leave again, and, being quite unable to imagine how G.M. would take a scene, or even a grim atmosphere, I telegraphed him, perforce at the last minute, to put him off. Anything would be better than 'a situation' I should never hear the last of. A few days passed, then came his letter: my telegram had arrived just as he was getting into a taxi for the station, and he ended with the words: 'No *explanations* or *apologies* are necessary.'

Marie Beerbohm came often a little later on and the three of us, with Deirdre reading absorbedly in a corner, had many a good talk, some of which was about that peculiar and charming T. W. Earp, whom Marie had recently met. He was often in Oxford and should certainly be invited to come here.

By now it was entirely autumn. Sybil having gone to London, I was alone with Deirdre for about a week and, during our daily care of the house (what a morning that was when we carried in as much dead wood as we could handle, in view of the 'save-coal'), I got to know her much better and loved her. Among other things, she seemed to me very steady

– at nine years old – and if one may use the word for a child (why not indeed?) she appeared to me very *integrated*, not in the least dispersed or vacillating in character. With Sybil I sometimes felt I was with several people, so rich her nature, so consuming her vitality. That physical energy too! 'I've cleaned the whole house!' were the words that met me bringing Marie Ozanne for the night to Bagpuize. Most visibly, she had.

As for her effect on Marie Ozanne – Marie with her puritanical ideas *then*, to whom so many people appeared '*quelqu'un d'extraordinaire*', with her 'Nancy, *attention aux hommes!*' of 1915 – Marie who had had full measure, it seems, of *me* to be astonished at. Now, and soon after, she had Sybil for her amazement and wonder. They were quickly sympathetic to each other.

What fluctuations there were in Sybil at that time, her mood now high and enthusiastic, now silent and absorbed. Brief comings and goings between Bagpuize and London were sometimes so sudden that she would not have enough money with her, and local transport during the war was often erratic. What matter? As if chance-borne, Sybil would be back: 'It was pouring with rain. A man appeared at the corner just when I didn't know what I was going to do, and he carried my bag and telephoned everywhere and found me a taxi. It was all rather complicated, and when I told him I had no money to give him, he said he didn't want any, anyway.' Chance-borne or charm-borne? Rash things to such characters are often no obstacle. 'Courage, always courage' says Barrie somewhere – and I have just come across these words of George Moore's in about 1887: 'We talked of the great fortune that always lies about waiting to be picked up by the adventurous.' How much Sybil – like all people of spirit – would have liked that theme.

At times she would talk to me a great deal about life, and about liberty of choice, and also about conscience, varying astonishingly in her point of view. And I would feel more and more that she, of all people, was meant to be free. One day her mind seemed made up about this too; the next, something in her reversed the decision. The war had, inescapably, an awful effect on us; gay as we were on the surface, never were we without the fear of someone's death. At times Sybil did seem '*une exaltée*'. Do you suppose it was this which first attracted and then kept Marie Ozanne close to her for years afterwards?

'My idea of death,' Sybil said to me once, 'I mean, this is how one ought to think about death: it's as if one were going to a lovely party. You pull the heavy curtains apart and find yourself in a room full of friends.'

After this I was alone for several days with Marie Beerbohm at Bagpuize when we would walk for miles across the fields towards the Downs in such a hush laid over everything that it seemed almost to have some particular meaning. It was then that Sybil was in anguish over Sidney Herbert going back to the front; she had stayed in London to be with him as much as possible. It turned a little cold at night, a little haunted, and Marie felt presences uneasily in the house that had become gaunt with autumn, and so slept one night in my bed. So early next morning came Sybil that I started up in fear that something awful had happened to her. She came straight in, stood by the bed a moment, and said very calmly and very clearly: 'Peter has been killed.'

We went to London that afternoon and the misery of the week that followed is not a thing that words can describe. It seemed to me that Sybil was suffering for *me*, too, in the midst of her great dread for Sidney; Peter's death and her fear for Sidney were now bound up together. Sidney came often to see her all those days where we were both in Mione's house. The long conversations behind closed doors, the atmosphere of some decision being taken and then reversed, made me very uneasy about her. She would talk much of Sidney; he was, I think, the one she would have been best, best and happiest with.

And then we went back to Bagpuize and were alone there, entirely alone with Deirdre, the whole of November. All this time was grey without and wretched within and, as it is impossible to find words for utter and total loss, when one longs to be dead too, and would be if one had the immediate courage of suicide, let me tell you one thought of Sybil's then which, although it may sound extraneous, contains the whole parabola of unhappiness; it describes that state when the mind is entirely possessed by its pain, yet unconsciously revolts against it: 'the *boredom* of grief'.

The fact of Peter's death set the seal on my decision: after the war I would never live again with Sydney Fairbairn; I knew now this was quite final. All this long time with Sybil and Deirdre in the country was a time of misery unrelieved by anything, with the Spanish flu all round us, and when the end of the war did come that 11th of November, we were just silently at Bagpuize with bitter thoughts, and I went that day for a long, long walk alone.

Soon now the lease came to an end, and because we thought we would go on sharing a house a little longer, I found a dreary almost suburban dwelling much nearer London, at Bury Green, Cheshunt, somewhere near Enfield. Damp and wan, ugly, gloomy and dull – no wonder

Deirdre recalls that 'we never the saw the sun there', from December 1st until February 1st. Nothing moved, save thoughts and unhappiness, in the bleak, blank, icy days at Bury Green. On 1 January 1919 Sydney Fairbairn came back from France and the talk was had in London that brought the marriage to an end, even if he did not realise it at the time. Maybe Richard came once to Bury Green; Sydney did for one night, but all his arguing was in vain and, if he thought of turning to Sybil for aid, or even comment, it was to a wall. To me she seemed at that time to be withdrawing into herself.

During the last few years of her life I never saw Sybil at all, which is partly accounted for by my being nearly the whole time in France. During those last years I thought of her as of someone in the grip of silence, solitude and austerity – as far as her inner life was concerned – and conscience-troubled (though why?) and self-tormenting. Though I had not been with her for so long, her death was the falling blade of a guillotine. To me, as a friend she was, and in memory has remained, *unique*. And also, remembering all, I owe Sybil more than I owe anyone: the liberation of myself, for it was she, indeed, who brought this about.

24 January 1955
At Portenhall, Bedford   Nancy Cunard

PART FOUR : INTO THE WILDERNESS

All her lovers have passed, her beautiful lovers have passed,
The young and eager men that fought for her arrogant hand.

V. SACKVILLE-WEST

[1]

MARIE OZANNE, who for the rest of my mother's life was to be her closest friend and wisest counsellor, was the eldest of the three daughters of a French Protestant clergyman, whose English was so good that he often preached in it for the benefit of English visitors in his Calais parish. The girls were equally bilingual, and this accomplishment made their fortune. When they were first grown up they had only one friend in England, but she was powerful – Miss Wyatt, headmistress of Heathfield, near Ascot, one of the leading girls' schools in the country. She suggested that they should start a finishing school in Paris, to which she would direct her wealthiest and most distinguished pupils. Nancy had been one of the first of these, and the very first of those favourites on whom Marie conferred what the other girls considered unfair advantages. So far as is known, none of the sisters ever had any love-life (though the youngest, Lydie, was believed once to have had a shadowy admirer), and this side of their lives was lived vicariously, through the adventures and misadventures of their former pupils. Lydie, the best looking and the most literary of the three, was always the girls' favourite. Alice, the middle sister, was the most business-like, energetic and efficient. Marie was considered by the others too impetuous, extravagant, and unorthodox. They all dressed with great *chic* and subdued style. To avoid constant visits to the hairdresser, all three habitually wore wigs, which looked remarkably natural, though a request in a theatre for one of them to take off her hat involved a stumbling journey to the cloakroom.

When the war came and Paris was threatened, the sisters moved their

Marie Ozanne

school to a large house in Charles Street, Berkeley Square, and it was from there that Marie came into our lives. She was plump, gay, generous, very fond of food but abstemious in drink. She loved the theatre, scandalous books, and above all the gossip of her friends (*'Barbara m'a raconté un tas de choses'*). My mother loved to tease and shock her. In a crowded Paris restaurant she would say in a loud voice: *'Voyons, Marie, toi qui as toujours deux hommes dans ton lit'*, and, refusing all food, would gradually eat most of Marie's. This unexpectedness continually surprised, delighted and scandalised Marie. We loved her always and she loved us, first as appendages of our mother, then I believe for ourselves.

Meanwhile, after I had gone back to school in September 1918 my mother's letters from Bagpuize came daily. Here are a few extracts:

Saw Wyndham Lewis for a minute. I hope I may get Ralph [Grimthorpe] to buy some wonderful new drawings he has done . . . I heard yesterday that another of my friends has been killed, Lord Alexander Thynne. I am so sorry about it . . . I sent you a pencil-sharpener, a little book which will do as a diary, two sections of honey, and pots of strawberry, raspberry, gooseberry and blackcurrant jam . . . I had lunch with Lewis, who said he would write to you. Deirdre has just gone off to the general shop to get some rolled oats and to enquire about a buck rabbit. I did love our afternoon together, my

little darling perfect son, and thought about you all the way back in
the taxi with so much love . . . I dined with Lewis, a friend of his called
Iris Barry who writes poetry and a married couple called Wadsworth
(he camouflages ships). Joker has turned out to be a buck. I had a talk
with Winston Churchill, who praised Uncle Duff enormously.

In the middle of October Sidney came home on fourteen days' leave,
and Sibbie spent most of it with him in London. Together they
welcomed Duff back from the war. Armistice Day at Stanmore was a
lugubrious affair. After singing God Save the King in the gymnasium we
mooched round the sodden playing-fields in a damp mist, while
maroons and church-bells boomed and rang all round us. And on
November 25 I wrote:

> Oh, my darlingest, *many, many* happy returns of the day. Fancy you
> being thirty-two now. Aren't you getting grown up! There are exactly
> twenty-one more days till the holidays. Please send me some jam and
> some fruit. I am reading *The Children's Iliad* and have just got to the
> part where Appolo showers down his arrows upon the Greeks.

And then, as if the oddly spelt god was still at work, the disease called
Spanish Influenza swept over Europe, carrying off in a few months more
victims than had fallen in the four years of war. Our beloved Aunt Steffie
died in her London flat in December, after only four days' illness, and as
the rest of the family mourned in London, Deirdre and I gloomily
cleaned out the rabbit-hutches at Bury Green and then decorated a tree
for this sad Christmas.

[2]

The war was over, but Sibbie's conflict was still unresolved. For most
of January 1919 she was in London with Sidney, desperately trying to
decide what to do when Richard came back for good at the end of the
month. Most of all she would like to be divorced and married to Sidney,
but she still refused to be parted from her children. Next best would be
to live with the children in a London flat, but Richard would never agree
to this, and anyhow where was the money to come from? The common-
sense answer was to go back and live in the same house with Richard: he
was prepared to take her back: her mother, who had been wonderfully
tolerant about her various escapades, urged her to take this course, and
so did Duff. But she viewed the prospect with horror, particularly since,

at least to begin with, it would mean rejoining Richard's parents in Kent.

On January 27 Richard arrived, and they had a long fruitless discussion in Lady Agnes's flat. Next day, as though feeling the tension at long distance, I wrote from Stanmore: 'The only thing that I am at all unhappy about is whether you are happy.' Long before I had heard of Oedipus I would gladly have murdered my father and married my mother.

On the 29th Duff reported her 'in a terrible state of depression, not having made up her mind what to do'. In the stress of anxiety she contracted influenza, mercifully not the virulent kind but serious enough for Ford's Hotel to turn her out. She spent a week in a nursing home, where Sidney visited her. And then, after a last futile search for a flat with her mother, on 25 February she surrendered to the inevitable and agreed to join Richard next day. That evening the prospect suddenly seemed insupportable and she attempted to kill herself with poison in Duff's flat. Sidney and Duff found her unconscious on a sofa and managed to find a doctor, who gave her an antidote. In the early hours of the morning she was sufficiently recovered to be taken back to her hotel.

Duff spent all the next morning with her and took her to lunch at the Berkeley – 'a dreadful meal: she never spoke'. Then, in despair and desolation she travelled down to Kent with Richard. Two days later she wrote to me: 'I came here the day before yesterday and we are going to live here. I hope you will be pleased, darling. You see it is much simpler and easier, as houses are so hard to get in London.' So were happiness and peace of mind.

[3]

Halcot (which my father soon renamed Halcot House, so as to sound less suburban) was near the village of Bexley in Kent. Originally built as the Dower House of nearby Hall Place (a Tudor house on earlier foundations, popularly believed to be haunted by the Black Prince and other notables) Halcot was a two-storey Queen Anne building with Georgian additions. It stood in a hundred acres of lawns, gardens, woods, a large walled kitchen-garden, and above the lawn a long wide terrace fronted by a stone balustrade said to have been rescued from the demolition of old London Bridge. My sister and I were indeed pleased at the idea of living there. Even with the old Hart-Davises still in occupation it seemed more *ours* than the Priory had ever done, and like most uprooted children we longed for a settled home. My father was able to commute daily to the City: the train-journey from Bexley took little more than half an hour. My mother bought a season-ticket (which she was continually mislaying) – a slender life-line from exile to lost delights. But to begin with she was sunk deep in misery, and her letters told of interminable games of bezique and patience with the old people, while Richard played the piano. She saw Sidney once in London, and thereafter kept her resolve to see him no more.[1] I was beginning to learn Greek at school; this reawakened her interest in the language, and I reported progress in my letters. Each term I told her what History we were doing: it began at different periods, but always seemed to end with Wars of the Roses.

Halcot

[1] In 1922 he was elected Conservative Member of Parliament for Scarborough and Whitby (succeeding Ger Beckett) and from 1923 to 1927 he was Parliamentary Private Secretary to the Prime Minister, Stanley Baldwin. But his health began to fail and eventually he was compelled to apply for the Chiltern Hundreds. He was made a baronet in 1936 and died in March 1939, aged forty-eight.

On 2 June Duff was married to Diana Manners at St Margaret's Westminster before a huge congregation. I proudly attended in my Eton suit and battered top hat, greatly envied by all the other boys. Off on their honeymoon they went, and back to the prison-house of Halcot went Sibbie. Soon she was plagued by deafness and splitting headaches, which were finally cured by visits to a specialist and a sojourn at Brighton. When Duff got home he went down to Halcot, thought it charming and was pleased that 'the reconciliation is proving a success'. Outwardly it was, owing to great efforts on both sides, and our month-long August holiday in a tiny house, 5 Channel View, on the front at Bexhill-on-Sea, went without a hitch. Each week we trekked across the town to the only shop that sold the *Gem* and the *Magnet*, two periodicals of which I was a fervent reader. One day on the beach, as Deirdre and I lingered with our spades and buckets, my father called cheerfully: 'Come on, you spawn of hell,' to which another encumbered father added: 'That's the stuff to give 'em!' Nancy came for the night and found the situation difficult, for Richard disliked and disapproved of her, but 'Sybil looking very lovely and golden; each time this particular quality of goldenness strikes me afresh'.

Sibbie and Deirdre at Bexhill

At the beginning of September I spent ten days at the home of a schoolfellow near Newark. This was the only time I was ever separated from my mother during any holdays, and although it was a lovely place and they were all extremely kind to me, I was not happy. Moreover I fell and cut my knee, but this turned out to be a blessing, since the wound became septic and caused me to miss the first weeks of the autumn term.

Meanwhile my mother was enjoying the first of many post-war visits to Paris. She travelled with Nancy, who recorded: 'a wild rush for the boat, leaping on to it somehow, regardless of luggage. Sybil, suddenly, carrying a wicker basket full of books and yellow knitting.' Most characteristic of her was her knitting – loose and gay and uncontrolled. No drabs or duns for her, but bright primary colours, yellow her favourite. An emerald green jersey she made for me lived on till 1971.

*Sibbie's passport photograph
1919*

In Paris with Marie Ozanne she went to theatres and restaurants – a delightful change from Halcot. The Ozannes had moved their school back, and it now occupied four flats, one above the other, in the Avenue Octave Gréard in the Champ de Mars, near the Eiffel Tower. Marie met my mother at the Gare du Nord, and as they sat sipping beer outside the little café opposite 'I adored Paris – the smell I know so well, the people, the streets, the old women crying *La Presse!*' She stayed at the Hôtel Lutetia in the Boulevard Raspail, saw Nancy, lunched with Marie at the Brasserie des Pyramides, where she had often eaten with Prydie before the war, and went to many plays, including Cecile Sorel in *L'Aventurière* at the Comédie Française. To cheer herself up she bought some gay red shoes, and the whole visit, as so often under the influence of Marie's affection and good sense, greatly raised her morale.

Back in London, Duff found her 'in wonderful spirits', and a few days later she was further cheered by the return to England of Iris, with her American husband Curtis Moffat, her son Ivan, a black nurse and a bloodhound. They all came to Halcot until they could move into one of the London houses that Lady Tree was forever decorating – 'gilded squalor' Iris called it. With the Moffats Sibbie saw *The Duchess of Malfi* and a play in which Viola Tree was acting. In her dressing-room afterwards Gerald du Maurier asked Sibbie if she thought she could dramatise Stevenson's *Master of Ballantrae*: she was tempted, but the idea came to nothing.

When I got back to school I was chiefly concerned with reading *The Thirty-Nine Steps* and with catching glimpses of the glamorous French heavyweight boxer Georges Carpentier, who was training near the school (on 4 December he won the European title by knocking out the British champion Joe Beckett in seventy-four seconds). At my mid-term exeat my mother took me to Drinkwater's *Abraham Lincoln*, which we both greatly enjoyed.

Somehow a Spanish teacher had been found near Halcot, and my mother studied with him several times a week. At the end of November she wrote: 'I feel dull and heavy in body and mind. However, I suppose I must pull up my socks and work a bit at my five studies – Spanish, Italian, Greek, Algebra, Logic.' For the last three she sat at the feet of a septuagenarian sage called T. A. Bowhay. He was sweet and gentle, with an extraordinary breadth of knowledge and a philosophical turn of mind. Three books of his were published after his death, of which *Life and Man* (1926), though almost impenetrable, was considered the most important. Sometimes my mother took Deirdre along. Mr Bowhay tried to teach her a new system of arithmetic of his own invention. It was entirely to do with dots and Deirdre never mastered it. He also attempted to teach her a little Persian to fill in the time.

By the end of the year Sibbie was beset by the hopeless depression which, with occasional bright intervals, was to weigh her down for the rest of her life, particularly in the autumn and winter. She longed to see Sidney again, but knew that she must not. Three diary-entries in an otherwise empty book describe the onset of this malady:

Friday night, 26 December 1919 The last few days have been full of miseries of many kinds: much remorse, great stagnation of the mind, and haunted by memories of things that can never recur. I awoke weary in mind and body, played golf with Richard and Rupert. There seems no elasticity in me nowadays, but a sort of sodden distress and a dreary bewilderment, occasionally alleviated by momentary relaxing when indulging in rest, food and drink, or playing some game which requires no effort of the mind. It almost seems the high road to idiocy at times, so must be striven against . . . Deirdre looks very lovely asleep tonight: her life must be good and happy.

29 December   It is a mild, bright morning, and I am struggling to shake off the clouds of depression and hopelessness, but seem to have so little initiative. This should not be a wasted day, and yet I know so well how it will be spent – taking the children for a walk, desperately playing memory games to keep them from quarrelling, lunch, hanging about, nothing read, nothing done. What is my work today? To keep the children well and happy, teach them all I can, show them a good example. I have been on a bad tack of late and have unbarred the gates of egoism. The monster has overwhelmed me. Courage.

31 December   I am feeling more than usually hopeless and inefficient today. The problem of the children worries me, perhaps un-necessarily much, but I feel them growing up and nothing done to make them like or do things that are beneficial to them. Every day seems spent in quarrelling, eating sweets, playing with silly toys, and there is an entire absence of discipline everywhere. Yesterday was an expensive and more or less wasted day in London. How does Duff keep so serene? He has the woman of his choice, and a career with regular work attached, which he has been taught how to do. That is it, I suppose. My head does not seem in a good state. I do nothing but smoke cigarettes and feebly scold the children.

Certainly at that time, when we were ten and twelve, Deirdre and I did quarrel a good deal in a tiresome, nagging way. At heart we were very fond of each other, but each felt some kind of jealousy: Deirdre because I was the elder, the favoured one: I because she, being always at home, saw so much more of our mother than I did. Gradually this minor animosity disappeared, until our mother's death united us in a bond of love and shared memories that will last till death.

[4]

In January 1920, at the end of the school holidays, my mother and I went to stay with my father's younger sister Audrey. She was pretty, gay, full of laughter and affection, but her husband Stuart Heaton, a farmer and farming expert, moved so often from one job or farm to another that she was condemned to spend much of her life in remote places, far from the company she so much enjoyed. Just now they were living at Knavesmire Lodge, York, overlooking the racecourse. Soon after they moved in they discovered the skeleton of a baby in the cistern of the downstairs lavatory: after much soul-searching and discussion they buried it in the garden at dead of night. Rain fell steadily during our visit, but we were absorbed by *Tarzan of the Apes* and its first sequels.

As soon as I had gone back to school my mother's depression returned.

During the next holidays we will do some Greek and also some drawing lessons. Deirdre has got tonsillitis and I a stye and a cold. I am reading one of Gorki's depressing books. I must read and write for several hours every day. This lethargy is increasing.

She caught the tonsillitis and was in bed for a fortnight, with a nurse in attendance. As though in sympathy I went down with influenza and spent most of the first half of the term in the sanatorium. In an attempt to cheer each other up we played word-games by post: who, without reference to books, could write down in ten minutes the most names of great men beginning with B (more and more of these games were played in the holidays, along with the exchange of quotations and the recital of poetry). Marie Ozanne showered us both with flowers, books, chocolates. She had a fund of (mostly depressing) French poetry, especially Victor Hugo, which she would recite without provocation: now to encourage recovery she sent my mother some jolly lines which ended:

> L'Ame à demi sous le linceul
> Que le silence charme seul
> Et que seul le rêve délivre,
> L'Ame habituée à souffrir
> Est trop vivante pour mourir
> Mais aussi trop morte pour vivre.

Iris weighed in with more penetrating but unanswerable questions:

I wonder what you think of all day in your bed with the bright green curtains and the half-blown skies outside – what sad thoughts, iron intentions, strange fantasies and embryonic longings weave their shawls about your shoulders and bring you perhaps no warmth for all your spinning.

A fortnight at Brighton with Richard and Deirdre completed her cure. She rode on the downs and consumed oysters and champagne at Sweeting's with Marie. 'Duff came on Saturday and was very nice. He had a violent argument with Richard about education and enjoyed some port wine.' Richard was now doing well in the City and had decided to buy Halcot from his parents: they were agreeable, but the day of their departure was several times postponed, so that on 27 March 'we all went to the polling-booth to vote this morning, but I found I have no vote after all, as I am only a lodger's wife. I was *furious*.'

My love of reading, learning and speaking poetry was steadily growing, encouraged by Duff's gift of a pound as a reward for reciting all Macaulay's 'Horatius' to him, and this June my mother copied out all three hundred lines of 'Charles Edward at Versailles' from Aytoun's *Lays of the Scottish Cavaliers*, so that I could learn them under the dormitory bedclothes with a torch. I did so, and they are still in my head, as so often happens with things absorbed of one's own free will at an impressionable age. Altogether during the next six years I learnt more than a hundred poems by heart, most of them short but some longish. After a time I could not remember exactly which I knew, so I entered them all alphabetically under poets in a tiny leather-bound address-book, and whenever my mother asked me to recite something I gave her the book to see what she would like. She was a perfect audience, and if this record seems well supplied with poetical quotations and allusions, that was the way we liked it.

My mother's letters of the early summer describe a visit to Madge and Walter at Westbury-on-Trym, and a grand luncheon party at Lady Cunard's, where she at last met and had a long talk with George Moore.

I have arranged for Deirdre to spend an hour a week with Mr Bowhay: since his marriage he has discarded his skull-cap and mittens, and wears a smart blue suit and tie. I loved the French play I saw yesterday, Sacha Guitry's *Pasteur*, wonderfully acted . . . I love the photographs of you, put one by my bed last night, kept on speaking to it, and *wished* you were here.

And then, after my exeat at home:

> I specially loved hearing you say [Kipling's] 'Mother o' Mine'. Did you do it thinking of me? I rather think so. Oh! my darling little son, I love you *more* than I can possibly say.

My reply, apart from endearments, was business-like:

> Yes, I did learn the poem thinking of you. The person who broke the greenhouse has not yet owned up. Please will you send *Dracula* at once.

Then came our first holiday abroad. For the month of August we rented the Villa Jean-Jeanne at Hardelot Plage, some ten miles from Boulogne. The Ozannes and a few of their pupils had villas there: we played tennis with some of them and made lifelong friends with K. and Nancy Tennant. The huge expanse of smooth sand in front and the open sand-dunes behind gave an impression of infinite space – a great improvement on the claustrophobic promenade at Bexhill. The local bigwig was Monsieur Louis Blériot, who in 1909 had been the first man to fly the Channel, and as we learned to bicycle on the sands we wobbled to and fro past his villa, hoping to see him emerge. Nancy had a villa there, in which we met her latest lover, a very polite and neatly dressed Armenian called Dikran: later that year he was to begin his meteoric literary career as Michael Arlen.

All the tennis and bicycling and bathing and meals at a rustic restaurant called the Pré Catalan were carried out against a background of steady explosions, as the huge Allied ammunition-dump at Etaples was methodically disposed of. As though this was not enough of a reminder, my father insisted on a motor-tour of the battlefields, so just before my thirteenth birthday we set off, my parents, myself and a City friend of my father's called Douglas Uzielli, in a hired car with a chauffeur (neither of my parents ever learnt to drive, nor did Duff). Relentlessly we explored the ruins of Ypres, Passchendaele, the skeleton villages, traversing seemingly endless miles of liquid mud covered with abandoned weapons and material of every kind, lined with the shockingly cut-off trunks of trees. The roads were mostly of planks laid laterally across muddy tracks, and where the inhabitants had taken the planks for firewood we had to get out and push. Uzielli, who was smartly dressed with spats, ended up covered with mud. My father enjoyed every moment. My mother was sickened by the thought that here or there one of her admirers might have met a hideous end. I collected a German helmet and bayonet, which were a great nuisance for the rest of the trip.

[5]

When we got back to Halcot we found that the grandparents had flitted, taking with them every fixture or fitting, every electric-light bulb, knob, handle or bracket they could detach, regardless of the elaborate list of such things that had been made long before. All they left were a dozen stags' heads which had threateningly surrounded the billiard-room. The ensuing wrangle rumbled on for months.

Now that the house was ours a great deal more furniture was needed, and some lovely old pieces were bought in Bristol by Madge, who had excellent taste in such matters. Extra servants were engaged, and when the tally was complete the staff, apart from several gardeners and a woodman, consisted of butler, footman, lady's maid, two housemaids, cook and kitchen-maid, all English.

The largest of the four sitting-rooms my father made into a music-room, for which he bought a second Blüthner grand piano. This was largely wasted, since he did not enjoy playing with amateurs, and professionals were either unwilling or too expensive. The person he most enjoyed playing with was Anthony Bernard, the conductor of the London Chamber Orchestra.

Two small sitting-rooms were knocked into one to form a library, where in the holidays I soon spent much of my time. My mother bought me a blank library-catalogue, in which I carefully entered particulars of all the books. In the column for publishers I repeatedly wrote names – Macmillan, Methuen, Heinemann and the rest – that became important to me in later years. My father had collected a large musical library. Besides biographies of composers, histories of music and *Grove's Dictionary*, he had acquired the complete works of his favourites – Handel, Bach, Mozart, Beethoven and Wagner – and had them all splendidly bound in leather. But except for *Der Rosenkavalier* and some Puccini his musical appreciation pretty well ended with Wagner. Once at a concert he startled the audience by exclaiming loudly during a pianissimo passage: 'Brahms was like Arnold Bennett: he had a fatal facility.' I never heard him play or mention Debussy, Sibelius, Elgar, Tchaikovsky or Mahler, let alone Ravel or Stravinsky. He had piano arrangements of everything he liked and played for hours at a time, often without an audience.

Such was the comfortable prison in which my mother spent most of the rest of her life. 'Never mind,' she wrote to Iris, 'a sweet dignity hangs about the forsaken when they are bowed but not bloody. The world is dull and grey today and I have been forced to listen to music unceasingly.' The only telephone in the house was in an awkward cupboard under the stairs. The only near neighbour was May, Countess of Limerick, a garrulous old Irishwoman who lived at nearby Hall Place and was by no means a kindred spirit. Iris came to stay, but it was an expedition to visit friends in London, or for them to come to Halcot. To begin with, my mother supervised the redecoration of the house, and then in desperation decided to join the Girl Guides, which meant passing tests in such things as knots and the Morse code, which she found very difficult. In November she escaped for a week to Paris, where she stayed with Marie.

From Stanmore, where I was now Head Boy, I sent reports on what I was reading (*Barnaby Rudge* and *The Mystery of the Yellow Room* by Gaston Leroux) and any snippets of news that might amuse her.

We now go out in groups to weed the cricket-pitch for next year with little forks.

We had a lecture on Monday by a person called Miss Bacon, about her adventures in balloons and airships. It wasn't *extraordinarily* good, but not bad.

Mrs Rothschild sent Mr Royle a present of twenty-four wild duck, and we are all going to have them for lunch tomorrow.

Today a boy (Williamson jun.) broke his leg in footer. He got his leg entangled with Mr Lee's who was playing, and it went snap. No more news. Tons of love.

At the end of the term my mother came down for the prize-giving and to watch my first performance on any stage in a small part in a one-act play by W. W. Jacobs called *The Ghost of Jerry Bundler*. Then we went happily back to Halcot for Christmas.

PART FIVE : MOTHER AND SON

All this still legible in memory's page,
And still to be so to my latest age.
                                        COWPER

THERE HAD BEEN talk of my trying for an Eton scholarship, but the
idea was dropped and instead I sat for the ordinary Common Entrance
exam and was placed in Remove, the highest possible form. This caused
some jubilation at Stanmore, and at Halcot, where Deirdre, perhaps in
an unconscious attempt to escape from the hopeless incompatibility of
our parents and my mother's misery, had begun to turn and live with
animals: she had birds and mice in cages, guinea-pigs, bantams, dogs,
and a donkey, all of which my mother had to look after if Deirdre fell ill.
For fun my mother entered Deirdre for a beauty competition for
children run by the *Daily Mirror* and she was awarded third prize (£10).
The old Hart-Davises thought this an undignified proceeding.

My mother's only escapes were periodical weeks in Paris, where Marie
spoilt her and paid for everything, or occasional days in London, which
were vitiated by lack of money. She was given one pound to cover the
whole day, every penny of which had to be accounted for. Deirdre
remembers many return journeys in the train, my mother desperately
trying, with a stub of pencil on a small piece of paper, to account for the
last few shillings.

My final term at Stanmore ended with prizes. These consisted of
leather-bound books, of which one had a modicum of choice. I achieved
Tennyson's collected poems, Creasy's *Fifteen Decisive Battles of the World*
and Macaulay's *Lays of Ancient Rome*, neatly dodging Sir John Lubbock's
Ants, Bees and Wasps, of which the school had clearly bought a job lot at a
discount. When my mother came to take me away she found me,
appropriately, in the sanatorium, 'looking very tall and white'.

Since we were almost always together during the holidays, there are
no letters to assist memory, which from that April recalls only Godfrey

Deirdre as prizewinner

Tearle in *Othello* and Gerald du Maurier in *Bulldog Drummond*. Also Deirdre and I began to have elocution lessons from a semi-retired actress called Laura Smithson: these proved useful to me later.

Then came my departure to Eton on 28 April 1921, after a tiring day visiting relations in London. Duff gave us an excellent lunch and presented me with a tiny Pickering edition of Horace, but all of them, in an attempt to cheer me up, said or implied that I was approaching the happiest days of my life. Feeling sure that this was not so, I remained glum and unconvinced. As we had an hour before catching our train, my mother asked whether I would mind paying a short visit to a friend of hers. By then I minded nothing, so we drove to Osbert Sitwell's house in Carlyle Square. He and my mother talked until it was time for us to go: Osbert said nothing to me, but as we left he silently pressed a ten-shilling note into my hand. Many years later I reminded him of this perceptive act of generosity.

In the train my mother took a deep breath and said: 'There's something I want to warn you about. The older boys in the school are almost grown-up men, ready to fall in love with girls. But there are no girls about, so they sometimes fancy they're in love with girlish-looking younger boys. This is a bad thing, and you must have nothing to do with it.' All of which seemed to me natural and sensible.

Although Eton was scarcely further away than Stanmore, my going there seemed to mark another stage in my growing up and being separated from her. On the day after my going she wrote:

> Darlingest, darlingest little son. How I do miss you! More than ever before. I have no heart for anything and feel very mopey. Everything here reminds me so of you, and I nearly cried when I went into your empty room and saw some dreadful detective stories lying about. I expect I shall get resigned and settled down soon, but at present it seems a crime to have you away from me for so long, and such lovely months too.

She was somewhat cheered by the arrival of her mother, who came for a six-months stay, bringing her own furniture. Lady Agnes – Granny Cooper to us – was a delightful little old lady, rather deaf but full of jokes and good advice. When I told her that I subdued my strong curly hair by dipping my head in cold water every morning she said: 'Darling boy, you're storing up years of neuralgia for yourself.' She and my mother always got on well, and her presence just now was a blessing.

Then came the Girl Guides. My mother succeeded in passing her Tenderfoot test, bought a uniform, and was installed as Captain of the First Bexley Troop, whose headquarters were established in a room above the stables. Knots and the Morse code were still difficult, but Deirdre, who was a member of the Troop, helped her out. Luckily she remembered most of her First Aid from the war, and when all else failed she staged a deathlike faint, to test the girls' reactions.

Meanwhile I was gradually settling in at Eton, where I had followed Duff to the house of E. L. Churchill. He was universally known as Jelly, though nobody remembered why. He was a bachelor of complete integrity, sometimes stern but always fair and prepared to listen. I grew to like and admire him more and more.

It was a glorious summer, and I loved bathing in a backwater of the Thames called Cuckoo Weir. I sent home a long description of the visit of the Crown Prince of Japan, when the whole school formed up in School Yard and shouted 'Banzai'. (When the Prince, a very small man, visited the Stock Exchange, the reiterated cry was 'Pick him up'.)

In June Duff and Diana drove down to see me, causing a sensation with their bright-yellow open Ford two-seater. We drove over to

Monkey Island and lay in the sun while Duff read aloud *The Plattner Story* and others by H. G. Wells. I only just got back in time for chapel. Everything went well for Eton that year: they beat Harrow and Winchester at cricket and won the Ladies' Plate at Henley. Clearly I had come to the right school.

Our summer holiday was again spent at Hardelot, this time in a villa called Les Diablotins. All such holidays were complicated by two of my father's idiosyncrasies. Always subject to insomnia, he declared that he could not sleep a wink if the smallest crack of light penetrated the curtains, which in most of the summer villas and hotels were flimsy and transparent. So immediate search had to be made for some efficient blackout-material and the means of fixing it in position. Secondly my father so much disliked shaving that he pretended he couldn't shave himself, which was patently nonsense, since he had had to do so all through the war, and it was not always easy in French resorts to find a barber who was prepared to come and shave him every day, including Sunday.

After we came home I saw my first Test Match, at the Oval, England against Warwick Armstrong's all-conquering Australians.

[2]

On 20 September my mother took me back to Eton for my second half. Almost as though she foresaw some disaster, the parting affected her more than ever before. After taking me to my house she had to wait some time for her train at Windsor, so she went to the Castle Hotel and wrote to me:

> It has all been so happy and perfect, darling, that there remains almost nothing to say, except Thank God for you. Be good and sweet and brave and kind, and rather clever if you can, and I shall always be happy. All my life is centred on you, and your success is mine. I shall and *do* miss you horribly, but I think of all our time apart as a sort of preparation to make me more able and fit to be your mother, to learn things and get nicer and more useful for you.

These passionate lover-like words might have placed an intolerable burden on many a fourteen-year-old boy, but I accepted them as perfectly natural, for that is how things were.

Within a few days the disaster she had sensed opened its attack. I began to have severe abdominal pains, was put to bed and examined by one of the school doctors. He could find nothing wrong with me and passed me fit to play football. I sent an S.O.S. to my mother, and on 25 September wrote:

> I am up today, but I have still got the pain. I'm longing to see you on Tuesday. Please bring my Bible and umbrella.

On the 27th she drove down to Eton and saw Churchill. She told him she was sorry if it meant my leaving Eton for good, but she was not satisfied with the doctor's diagnosis and intended to take me up to London immediately to see a specialist. Jelly unwillingly capitulated and she took me straight to a nursing home at 6 Bulstrode Street, off Welbeck Street, where Duff visited me. The specialist was a large and rather too genial surgeon called Girling Ball. He confessed himself baffled by my pain but concluded that it was probably caused by an inflamed appendix. Our dear Dr Furber was not convinced by this argument, but in default of any other ideas my appendix was removed on 4 October and found to be perfectly healthy.

After a few days the pain returned and my mother became distraught. She was staying with Duff and Diana, and caused them a great deal of worry and annoyance. She began to drink more than she could tolerate, made a vain attempt to see Sidney, and moved to the Cavendish Hotel. Duff and my father feared for her reason.

On 18 October I had my second operation, an exploratory one that discovered an internal abscess. They drained it and sewed me up again. Next day my mother agreed to take a room in the nursing home and undergo some kind of rest-cure. She stayed there as long as I did and gradually regained her balance. We were now so close, in every sense, that she suffered with me when I was in pain and rejoiced with me when I felt better. She asked everyone she could think of to write to me. Jelly Churchill wrote long letters full of Eton football news. Dear Walter Crum sent me a tiny photograph of the Rosetta Stone with a letter that might have been written in the Stone's hieroglyphs. Most of the others wrote a kind perfunctory letter or two, but one man shone out in kindness. This was the novelist Stephen McKenna. He barely knew my mother and had never seen me, but he immediately responded to her call for help, sent me a present of a red leather despatch-case, and wrote me twenty-one letters, almost daily from 27 October to 28 November. At the beginning of this time he was setting out on a lecture-tour in Sweden and Denmark, but before he left he wrote to my mother: 'I have been trying to find a quotation for you, and I cannot. It is to this effect: "To bear my son I looked death in the face." To that you must add: "To keep him I looked death in the face again." Whatever has to be done must be done by you. If you feel fortified by knowing that others are thinking of you and trying to cheer you on, it will not matter that you do not hear their voices. Don't doubt and don't fear.'

His letters to me, first from London, then from shipboard, Gothenburg, Stockholm and Copenhagen, then from London again, were long and amusing, full of funny stories, puns, and a detailed account of his lecture-tour, and his later adventures in England. Many years later I was able to thank him for his extraordinary kindness.

When my pain returned yet again, and the doctors were still baffled, my mother felt sure I was dying, as indeed seemed probable to all, for I was by now so emaciated that my bones appeared to be covered by nothing but a thin layer of skin. To cheer me and to procure a likeness she asked Augustus John to come and make a drawing of me. This he obediently did, producing four drawings in an hour, tearing up two and giving us the other two. He was then at the height of his power as a draughtsman.

Rupert by Augustus John

Many other visitors, known and unknown, arrived at Bulstrode Street. Goodness knows how or where my mother came across a self-styled bishop, who visited me adorned with robes of his own designing and attempted to interest me in what I now suppose was some form of Theosophy. But I was in no state to relish such ministrations, and when he began trying to give me the kiss of life I told my mother he must never come again.

Finally in desperation Girling Ball decided he must operate again if my life was to be saved. He did so on 31 October and found another abscess. This time he left the wound open, with two short pieces of rubber tubing in it. These had to be taken out, sterilised and re-inserted every day: an agonising process usually heralded by Ball's loud voice joking with the nurses on the stairs. Miraculously this treatment succeeded, and very gradually I grew stronger and even optimistic. Duff came to see me regularly, and on 13 November he recorded: 'Went to see Rupert, whom I found wonderfully well. He is so nice and so nice-looking. Sibbie was there, looking awful.'

But as I recovered, so did she, and her main occupation now was keeping me amused. She read to me tirelessly, but as laughing hurt me we tried to avoid anything funny. One day, as she was reading in a book about cricket a long passage about preparing the pitch, the sight of her deliberately solemn face gave me agonising giggles, in which she reluctantly joined. She bought me books, jigsaw-puzzles, and above all, conjuring tricks, at which with much practice I became quite skilful. Once she left a shop with some tricks that were reserved for members of the Magic Circle. The manager of the shop pursued her into the street, telling her she couldn't do such a thing, but she told him that my needs were greater than the Magic Circle's and escaped with them. I gave shows to all the friends whom my mother persuaded to visit me, and so we both slowly got back to something like normal, and were able to return to Halcot in an ambulance shortly before Christmas.

[3]

For the first five months of 1922 I recuperated happily at home, and my mother was tranquil and happy because we were together. I had grown considerably during my illness and was now more than six foot tall. First I went about in a bath chair, drawn by Deirdre's donkey, but was soon well enough to bicycle. My father, although he hated the game, believed that golf was good for his health, and we were all obliged to play with him. I detested it and never played again after I had left home. I was much occupied in stamp-collecting, mostly by post through the *Bazaar, Exchange and Mart*, in which Deirdre did a brisk trade in bantams and racing pigeons. I also began to collect the many works of E. Phillips Oppenheim, of which I could never get enough.

At the end of February my mother and I spent a fortnight at Bournemouth, first in the Branksome Towers Hotel, then at Canford Cliffs. We walked and played and went to the cinema. Deirdre was at home with a governess.

17 March was a very special day, with a visit to London, where I bought 177 stamps and we saw the original productions of Galsworthy's *Loyalties* and Barrie's *Shall we join the Ladies?* In April Deirdre and I played tennis and did a lot of bird's-nesting, in May we saw Gerald du Maurier in Barrie's *Dear Brutus*, and on 10 June I sadly returned to Eton for the summer half.

Having been automatically moved up twice during my absence I was now in the Upper School, but was told I must do one more half's fagging. Much of this I avoided by taking my work to the peaceful School Library, which only Uppers might use. Jelly and the Dame (Miss Buckland, the matron) were terrified of my getting ill again, and I was put to bed at the least sign of a cold in the head. I took full advantage of this indulgence. On 21 June I wrote to my mother:

> If you can manage to go to Winchester [for the Eton match] please write *at once* to Jelly and ask if you can take me. Don't make it look as though it was only me that wants to go (although it is) because he will think I am trying to avoid the Boy Scout field-day, which is on the same day.

This ruse proved successful. I enjoyed playing cricket and swimming at Ward's Mead, but directly I arrived home for Long Leave in the middle of July I contracted influenza and that was the end of my summer half. Despite a course of treatment from a London osteopath I remained feeble, but I was always happy with my mother, and now some of the stubs in her cheque-book made me laugh:

23 May 1919	Carmichael. A bit of a swindle. £4.19.0
10 Jan 1921	Winter. Wasted on toys. £4.16.9
26 Jan 1922	Diseased old 1919 bantams – beastly. £1.5.0

And in my father's cheque book, in her writing:

30 Aug 1922   My dear wife, to balance overdraft. £20

Normally untidy, she would periodically make drastic clearances, once tidying the medicine-cupboard by swallowing all the remaining pills and draughts from almost-empty bottles.

The Halcot menagerie had been enlarged by the arrival of an enormous blue Borzoi of much grace and intelligence, the gift of a stranger met in the train. This creature was enlisted as the Girl Guides' mascot, but his atavistic habit of mistaking other dogs for wolves and holding them down by the neck caused so much local animosity that eventually he had to be given away.

But there were other and unusual visitants. I was only vaguely aware of them at the time, but Duff recorded how he and Diana drove down for dinner on 25 July:

At dinner, besides Sibbie, Richard and the children, were Dick Twining [my father's partner] and his wife, and a Miss Mellor, who, we were told, was a great spiritualist. We had a good dinner, and after the children had gone to bed we were told of a series of most incredible events which were said to have taken place in the house during the last few days. Miss Mellor, a fat comfortable-looking, complacent woman, explained that the garden was haunted by evil spirits who were endeavouring to get into the house.

Several queer things had happened. Two nights before, when Dick and his wife were in bed, Dick says that something happened like an explosion near his head. He swears he was awake at the time. Immediately afterwards strange coloured lights began flashing about the room, playing particularly round a picture of the Virgin Mary. He woke up his wife and they both sat up in bed for some time watching the lights. At last they could bear it no longer, so he went for Miss Mellor, who came and exorcised the spirits with signs and prayers.

On the following night she, Richard and Dick were sitting at the dinner-table finishing their port after dinner, when something took place which precipitated Dick from his chair on to another, and left Richard like a man suffering from shell-shock. Miss Mellor again came to the rescue and finally restored him. Her explanation was that he was temporarily possessed by a devil.

The whole thing is incredible, but there is no doubt that they all firmly believe it. What is most strange is that Sibbie, whom one would expect to be the centre of anything of the sort, has less to do with it than any of them and is apparently not much interested. Richard informed Diana afterwards in the strictest confidence that the medium must be Sibbie, that she was always wandering in the garden at night, that all the spirits came from the garden, that at times he saw other people look out of her eyes, and that a dog which she has recently acquired – a large Borzoi – was also in league with the evil things. When I heard this I wondered whether Richard was losing his sanity – and I still do wonder. The whole atmosphere of the place was strange and uncanny.

A few days later, untroubled by these spirits from the vasty garden, my mother, Deirdre, the Borzoi and I travelled again to Branksome Towers, where we spent a month. In the middle we all went for a week-end to Brighton, where we watched Middlesex *v.* Sussex and bought a Pekingese puppy, which was luckily too small to interest the Borzoi as prey. Back in Bournemouth I watched three Hampshire matches. We several times drove over to visit Augustus John and his family at Alderney Manor, where Deirdre was badly kicked by a horse. Doctors diagnosed an injury to the base of the spine, with possibly frightening consequences, but my mother, always ready to try anything new, called in a lady faith-healer who was staying in the hotel; she immediately removed the pain, and all was soon well. Then, after a few days at home, we crossed once more to Hardelot and spent three weeks with the Ozannes.

[4]

As I had been away from school for almost a year, my return in September was more than usually distressing. And my mother felt the same: 'I have felt very low-spirited since you went away, quite like old times. Can't shake it off.' At Eton my extreme homesickness was aggravated by an almost constant cold in the head and feeling of exhaustion. Football was an ordeal, for, although my large abdominal wound had healed, it was tender and I was terrified of being kicked on it. Desperate letters to my mother brought her to the rescue. She had a long talk with Jelly and persuaded him to excuse me football and Early School. Even so, and despite huge food parcels from London and frequent visits from my mother, I continued to feel ill and miserable. 'I don't think you realise how *perfectly lovely* home is, until you have been in some comfortless place like this.' We were not allowed fires in our rooms till the end of October, and then only every other day, though Jelly and the Dame were kind according to their lights.

Nor was my mother feeling much more cheerful. On 16 October she wrote:

> My most loved and precious boy. I do love your letters so; they are my one joy these days, for I must admit quite privately to you that my spirits are far from good . . . Forgive this gloomy letter. After all you and I must pour out our troubles to each other, and then we get better.

Not least of her troubles were the Girl Guides, whom she found increasingly tedious. After a penitential conference of Commissioners in Derbyshire she sent in her resignation, but was somehow, against her will, persuaded to soldier on. She went to see Dr Furber, who gave her 'some mixed monkey glands' and told her that her blood-pressure was abnormally low.

I entered for an English Literature prize, for which, curiously enough, we had to read an abbreviated translation of *Don Quixote*. My mother read it too and we compared notes, finding that neither of us had enjoyed it much. Her mother came to Halcot for a month, and at the beginning of November I went home for the Long Leave week-end, which a perpetual cold, sore throat and high temperature extended until it was too late for me to go back to school. How many of the symptoms were unconsciously self-induced so that I could stay at home is impossible to say, but the good Dr Hinds did his best to allay them. He was a dear old country doctor with crooked pince-nez, very anxious to please. Each of his innumerable visits ended with my mother asking what I could have to eat, and his reply always began 'Soup, a little fish if there is any . . .' Eventually my mother could bear this formula no longer: 'What do you mean "if there is any"? The house is full of fish.' Similarly in London Dr Furber did his best to fall in with her wishes. At the end of November, after he had hemmed and hawed about my condition and realised that my mother was not satisfied, he asked, 'What do you want me to say?' And when she suggested a fortnight at Brighton he readily agreed.

At Brighton we read *The Wrong Box* aloud, revelled in Martin Harvey in *The Only Way* and Maeterlinck's *Burgomaster of Stilemonde*, and spent much time with the slot-machines on the two piers. The only way I could be persuaded to take any exercise was by being promised a visit to Combridge's secondhand bookshop opposite Hove town hall. And so, with a visit to Arthur Bourchier in *Treasure Island* in London, this year of illness and truancy came to an end.

[5]

I felt so ill and homesick at Eton at the end of January 1923 that my mother came twice in one week to see me, before spending a fortnight in Paris with Marie Ozanne. I was in bed in the sickroom with a nurse for the second half of February, and my mother was in the same state at Halcot, where 'Dr Hinds says I am not to have any curries, entrées, Worcester sauce or Brazil nuts. P.S. The lady where Grace is now is called Mrs Coldtart.' Back at Eton after another Long Leave protracted by illness, I consoled myself by reading *Wuthering Heights* and the ghost stories of the Provost, M. R. James. And then came news of a journey that was to have unexpected consequences. On 16 March my mother wrote: 'I am going to fly from London to Paris tomorrow. Pray to St Christopher for my safe journey over the water. He is the saint for that sort of thing.'

This was her first flight since looping the loop with Hamel in 1914, and no doubt St Christopher's protection came in useful.

We had quite a good journey till one of the carburettors burst and something caught fire. However, all was well and we made a good landing in a field near Abbeville, quite close to the railway line. We were considering walking to Abbeville station and getting the next train, when another machine hove in sight, picked us up and conveyed us to Gay Paree. I enjoyed the flying very much, especially the last part in the French machine, which went much higher – 5000 ft instead of 2000. I wasn't the least nervous, except just at first.

She stayed with the Ozannes, where their doctor said that her bronchial tubes were in a bad way and ordered her to bed. After a few days the Ozannes had to take a party of girls to Italy, so my mother moved to the Hôtel Meurice, accompanied by an Irish Catholic Nurse Conway. There she was visited by several friends, including Robert Siegfried, who had proposed to her when she was fifteen.[1] An osteopath helped her recovery, and she was soon well enough to champion the cause of her sister Steffie's elder daughter Violet. After their mother's death she and

[1] He died later that year, aged forty. In 1925 three essays of his were published as *Lettres et Discours sur les Passions.*

her sister Enid had become wards of an uncle whom they detested: Violet was now miserably unhappy at a finishing school in Paris. She called to my mother for help, saying, truthfully, that her uncle had made quasi-amorous approaches to her. My mother, horrified, removed her from the school and took her to the Meurice. The school reported her absence, and her uncle arrived from London with a detective called Joseph Madigan. Violet repeated her accusation in front of the British Consul General, who must have been puzzled as to what he was expected to do. Eventually Violet went back to England and was never molested again. On 2 April my mother wrote:

> I expect to leave Paris this morning. Violet's uncle is behaving in a very extraordinary way. I fear he is a bully and very Prussian in his methods. Violet is terrified of him, and I hope I shall be able to take her away from him, poor child. The Scotland Yard detective is a charming man and tells me thrilling stories about his various adventures. He caught Gerard Lee Bevan [an absconding financier].

And then, at the end of this same letter, almost as a postscript, she added:

> Last Friday I was rechristened and received into the Roman Catholic Church. It is a source of the greatest help, comfort and joy to me.

PART SIX : THE CLOISTER AND THE HEARTH

'Dost thou not love me, Lord, or care
    For this mine ill?' –
'I love thee here or there,
    I will accept thy broken heart – lie still.'

CHRISTINA ROSSETTI

SHE HAD FOR some time meditated such action, but the final step was taken, as so often with her, on a sudden impulse. Somehow she persuaded the Passionist Father Vincent Logan of St Joseph's church in the Avenue Hoche to receive her without any of the mandatory instruction.[1] When he rechristened her she took an additional Christian name, and in future signed herself Sybil Mary Magdalen. Directly she got home she went for instruction to Father Fabian Dix at the Dominican Priory on Haverstock Hill. When she told him what had happened in Paris he strode about the room in rage, saying, 'The priest who did that ought to be kicked.' To which she replied: 'Father Fabian Dix, if everyone got what they deserved, you and I might not be here.' At which he laughed and calmed down. She described him to me as 'a fiery, outspoken fellow and a wonderful preacher.' His instruction seemed to her inspired.

I naturally rejoiced with her in the happiness of her conversion, but when she again and again wrote: 'I do so wish you were a Catholic. Do you think you ever will be? It would make me very happy,' I sadly felt that such a decision must come from an inner conviction (which I lacked), and not simply from a desire to please the beloved. This was the only time I disregarded her wishes.

The nearest Catholic church to Halcot was at Crayford, a few miles away. It was a tiny hut of a building, presided over by a darling old Irish

[1] It was the Passionist Father Cuthbert Dunne from this same church who received Oscar Wilde into the Church on his deathbed in 1900.

priest called Father Carroll. He was a short elderly man with a round red face, pince-nez, and a slight stammer. He had decided views on literature: to him Bernard Shaw was Antichrist, and G. K. Chesterton a prophet sent from God. He used to lend me heavy volumes on the *History of Ethics*, which I did my best to read. He and my mother were devoted to each other, and she, together with his housekeeper, nursed him tenderly through his last illness in 1926.

Father Carroll

At first, with all the fervour of a convert, she went to Mass every day, several times on Sunday. 'You would have been amused to see me doing the flowers in the church this morning. I kept crashing into things and upset some Communion wine . . . I cleaned all the brasses in the church.' Soon she became a Handmaid of the Blessed Sacrament, and of all her impulsive decisions her conversion was one that she never regretted.

[2]

In May she visited her old love Wyndham Lewis at a studio in Adam and Eve Mews. Deirdre had been decorating her lesson-books with funny little drawings, and my mother thought she would benefit from a lesson or two. Lewis agreed to give her one, and while he and my mother talked, Deirdre sat miserably trying to draw a rose in a glass. She achieved little except a blur of erasures, and was so discouraged by this experience that she never attempted to draw anything again.

Sibbie and Deirdre at Halcot

New friends were Sir Denison Ross and his wife. He was Professor of Persian in London University and Director of the School of Oriental Languages, a jolly man with an eye for a pretty girl. His wife, a forbidding and rather grubby-looking lady, was a considerable pianist, and was grudgingly allowed to play pieces for two pianos with my father.

Meanwhile my daily letters from Eton were loving but dull: 'I am reading *The Mysterious Affair at Styles* by a new writer called Agatha Christie. We had a sermon this morning from the Provost. I think his ghost stories are better than his sermons.' And for the Fourth of June my mother and Deirdre stayed in lodgings at Eton for four days. When I suggested going for tea to an hotel we had been to before, my mother said: 'No, no. The strawberries there look as though they've been combed out of old men's beards.'

Two days later I received a cry of distress:

> I got very badly ticked off by Daddy about money. I had cashed two cheques for £5 and one for £8–10 at Eton, and couldn't explain how I had spent it, except for £9–15–7. Can you remember or account at all for the remainder? Do help me if poss. I got very wretched and cried and put off going out with Uncle Duff tonight, but then Daddy became very kind and insisted on my going after all, and took me with him to the train and gave me £2 and a cigarette. I really must try to be better about money, and you must help me, please. These rows are so dreadful, and Daddy said I couldn't go to Eton any more, as I spent so much.

To which I triumphantly replied: 'I enclose a complete list of what you spent, which accounts for every penny. Show the list to Daddy, and I'm sure it will be all right.' So it was, but similar rows, mostly about trivialities, continued. I often telephoned to her once and even twice a day from an Eton hotel or shop to cheer her up.

The Girl Guides too were a constant worry. In the middle of June she was bidden to a Camp Conference for senior Guides at Eynsford in Kent. Despite official objections she insisted on taking Deirdre with her.

> We arrived just before eleven, put up our tent and some of the others, had some sandwiches for lunch, then put up another tent and our own camp-beds. It is *pouring* with rain and we *long* to be safely back at home. All the Guides are very jolly in the worst sense of the word. [*Next day*] We messed about, had dinner (cold ham), then had a very boring time round the camp-fire, then went to bed. It was very wet and blowy all night, and our palliasses were full of earwigs. We were up early and had the 'colour party' at eight. Then breakfast (bread and butter and tea). Then I had to saw wood and carry some terribly heavy buckets of water up a hill all the morning. After lunch we felt we couldn't stand it any more, so telephoned for a car to wait at the end of the road, and crept out during the siesta-hour.

Next day she wrote: 'I am haunted by the Guides and wish to goodness the "Movement" had never been thought of.'

In July we persuaded my father, much against his will, to come to the Eton and Harrow cricket-match at Lord's. He sat in glum silence, smoking cigarette after cigarette. When a newcomer in the row behind tapped him on the shoulder and said: 'Excuse me, sir, but can you tell me how the last wicket fell?', he answered: 'It fell from sheer *ennui*.'

At the end of the month I went home for the holidays and found

Lady Agnes in old age

Granny Cooper staying there. Duff came down and recorded: 'Mother there. Sibbie quiet, Richard argumentative, Rupert tall, Deirdre beautiful.' A week later we set off, Granny and all, for Etretat on the Normandy coast, but after a few days my mother began to suffer agonising toothache. A dentist in Havre proved useless, so my mother and I travelled by train to Paris, where an American dentist put things right. We ate lavishly at Voisin's and the Grand Vatel, visited the Musée Grévin and the stamp-market in the Champs Elysées before returning to Etretat. The weather was appalling, the sea mountains high. An employee of the casino went in for a bet and was dashed to death on the shingle. When we asked a local how they would ever recover the body, he said they would wait a few days and then go up the coast to Fécamp, where they would surely find it. 'We may find a few others there too,' he said; 'all the bodies are washed up there.'[1]

On a calmer day we watched the great Suzanne Lenglen play an exhibition tennis match, and every evening we played *boule* in the casino, but it was a dreary holiday and we were glad to get home.

[1] Swinburne was very nearly drowned at Etretat in 1868.

Back at Eton I was again excused football, and played a good deal of squash instead. In an attempt to keep me well I was given another room, next door to the boiler and so less arctic than most, but I immediately caught a heavy cold, which persisted, off and on, for the rest of the year.

[3]

In October my mother was confirmed by the Bishop in St George's Cathedral, Southwark, and shortly afterwards attended a Retreat at Grayshott in Surrey.

Father Bede Jarrett gave us an address. He is wonderful. I simply *love* being here and expect I shall become a nun some day, when you no longer need me. I hope to be much better after the Retreat and am forming many good resolutions.

To which I answered:

I don't want you to become a nun, darling, and I shall *always* want you and love you oh so much. I am taking pure cod-liver oil twice a day now.

As a preacher and public speaker in the Catholic England of his time Father Bede Jarrett was unique. Born in 1881 he became a Dominican at seventeen and was ordained priest in 1904. He took Firsts in Mods and History at Oxford and studied theology at Louvain. Prior at Haverstock Hill from 1914 and English Provincial of the Order from 1916 to 1932 (the longest tenure recorded), his crowning achievement, in which he wore himself out, was the return of the Dominicans to Oxford, whence they had been banished by the Reformation. Three houses in St Giles (one of them Walter Pater's) were converted into Blackfriars Priory and opened in 1929. Three years later Father Bede was appointed Prior there. After his death in 1934 his old Oxford tutor Sir Ernest Barker wrote: 'I have often thought that I learned more from him than ever he learned from me . . . He had a great candour and a gentle modesty; a noble person and a memorable voice; a gift of wise and eloquent instruction; a knowledge of learning and a power of giving counsel by understanding.'

It was to this most human of saints, first at Grayshott and then at St Dominic's, Haverstock Hill, that my mother poured out the story of her life, her mistakes, sorrows and regrets, her fears for the future, and her gratitude for her new-found faith. Under his instruction she read a great

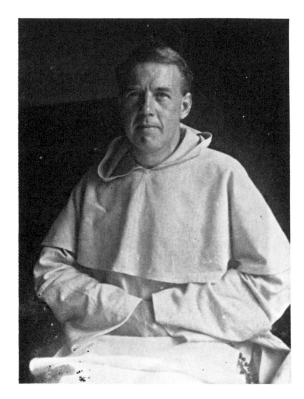

Father Bede Jarrett

deal about the Order, even delving as deep as the works of the fourteenth-century Dominican Meister Eckhart. After her death Father Bede wrote:

> I must own that I discouraged her, as I could see – it wasn't so very long before her illness came down on her in its full fury – that with her it might so easily become an obsession and develop into a great fear. Her nature was so intense and concentrated that one dreaded her interest in the things of the Faith, at the beginning of her Catholic life. One preferred she should go quietly at first, and then later on develop her spiritual life with growing interest.
>
> But I think she was one of those who are not so much interested in life, human and divine, as consumed by it, to whom religion is not so much a light as a flame. She was burnt up by that fire within.
>
> Alas that I didn't know her well enough to gauge that courage of which Wilfrid Meynell speaks; she certainly had all the glow that illuminates courage and that docility of mind that seems so often and so surprisingly to march side by side with it. It was only in little ways

that I was able to see the force, directness, and kindness of her character, and her sympathy with all spiritual efforts and distress.

She several times took me to hear Father Bede preach, and I too fell, to a limited degree, under his spell. After my mother's death he wrote me, in the midst of his extremely busy life, a number of wise, interesting and compassionate letters. A wonderful man.

[4]

At the end of November my Aunt Mione died at Wiesbaden in Germany. Her life had been troubled and aimless, her marriage a failure. My grandmother was with her at the end, much puzzled by the exchange, which stood at several million marks to the pound and was constantly changing. Although my mother had not seen much of Mione for years, her death brought sorrow: 'I keep remembering all sorts of times and things about her long ago when we were quite little, and it seems difficult to realise she is dead. I have *no* sisters now.' However, there was one little compensation: her mother was now able to increase her annual allowance from £200 to £400.

On the eve of her thirty-seventh birthday she wrote: 'Tomorrow I am to go to London to try and choose a fur coat. Daddy says I can spend the £40 he won at chemin-de-fer on it.' And next day:

Our train to London this morning was nearly an hour and a half late on account of the fog. Daddy got maddened and smashed a glass in the carriage over a map. I chose my fur coat. It is made of moleskin, very warm and neat, I think. Price 65 guineas!![1] The vet says the parrot will soon die, so the thing is to get it safely back to Gamages before it does.

In December she crossed to Paris to spend a few days with her mother, who was on her way from Germany to the South of France. They stayed together at the Hôtel Meurice, where my mother wrote:

Mon petit chéri. Merci pour tes gentilles lettres. J'espère que tu vas bien et que ton méchant rhume est fini. Il me semble que tu as beaucoup de travail en ce moment avec ces Trials. Ne te fatigue pas trop, et surtout ne te fais pas de mauvais sang. Tu es très intelligent et tu arrives toujours à faire ce que tu as à faire en fait d'examens etc.

[1] She eventually gave this coat to a female Russian refugee whom she met in a train and never saw again.

Je suis très heureuse içi à Paris, ma ville préférée entre toutes, et Maman est *si* contente de m'avoir près d'elle, la pauvre. Je l'aime tant, et mon coeur est si touché de la voir si seule et vieille, et cependant si joyeuse de nature, si généreuse et toujours pleine de courage pour faire ce qu'elle doit faire. Elle s'en va demain dans le Midi, et alors je vais m'occuper de mes cadeaux de Noel, et de tes timbres, mon amour.

Ne sois pas trop furieux de recevoir ma lettre écrite en français: il faut bien que tu apprennes cette langue, tu sais. Je vais tous les matins à la Messe et je fais bien des prières pour toi et pour ton bonheur, mon fils adoré. Je t'embrasse tendrement. Maman

The most I could do to live up to these expectations was to come top in Latin and to receive the *Collected Poems* of Rupert Brooke as a prize from my division master A. S. F. Gow. I also determined to specialise in French and German as soon as possible.

[5]

In January 1924 my father took an agreeable London house, 8 Wilton Street, for two months – a happy release from the boredom of Halcot. My mother determined to learn Hebrew, so as to read the Bible in what Coleridge's father called 'the immediate language of the Holy Ghost'. Denison Ross arranged lessons for her at the School of Oriental Languages, and soon she was gaily writing: 'I can now say nearly all the Lord's Prayer in Hebrew. I love you. I love you. Peace. Shalôm [Four Hebrew characters] Your v. loving Biddie the Yid.'

Then she was accepted as a novice in the Third Order of St Dominic, whose members are lay men and women, with novitiate, rule, and white Dominican habit, 'which must *not* be worn in public without permission of bishop and order'. This becoming garment was made for her by the nuns of the Dominican convent at Torquay, where she stayed for a few days. On the way there:

In the train I was just about to devour a delicious wing of chicken and some excellent ham, when I remembered it was Friday, so regretfully desisted and contented myself with some bread and cheese. At Torquay I had three bumpers of Kia-Ora and a tongue sandwich by mistake. I had bitten into a second one when I once again remembered it was Friday and dropped it like a hot coal.

The nuns worked quickly, and only a few days later 'I went to the convent to try on my habit. It looked awfully nice and all the nuns kept kissing me. Masses of love from your v. loving Novice.'
Back in London her religious life continued:

Low Mass at Westminster Cathedral. I put a *tiny* bunch of scarlet anemones at the feet of a large statue of the Sacred Heart and an even tinier one of white wood-hyacinths in the hand of a Pièta. Deirdre said everyone stared at me with amazement. After lunch to St Dominic's Priory to attend my first Chapter Meeting, which I liked tremendously. We Tertiaries were all given cards at random with a saint to devote ourselves to especially this year and try to imitate. I got St Cecilia, bless her.

London provided other small interests and pleasures:

Audrey came and took us to see a very old woman called Hancock, who said Deirdre will squint if she doesn't look out and I may have a goitre, but she will soon cure us!

She enjoyed *The Immortal Hour* and *The Dream of Gerontius*, met again her old friend Wilfrid Meynell, and saw a good deal of Iris, who was now obsessed by a bald and silent Serbian sage called Mitrinovic. Iris wrote to me in February: 'I went to the Coliseum the other night with your mother, Richard, the Twinings and the Serbian. A great many Scotch songs, which were met with our silent and Richard's audible expostulations.' A few days later my mother wrote:

I went with Iris to 28 Mallord Street and had lunch with the John family – Augustus, Dorelia and Romilly. The lunch was good, neatly set out in the kitchen. John was rather morose and exaggeratedly a great man, affecting high aloofness. I am in my nun's habit this evening: it is warm and soft.

And as the lease of Wilton Street came to an end and she prepared to return to the eternal sameness of Halcot:

I love your strong opinions about things: they are very helpful to me. I am so inclined to love everyone and have *so* little judgment. I am sorry about the stampless letters, but the servants all go to bed early with the stamps. I will write again tonight. This is just to tell you how tremendously I love you. You are the joy and comfort of my life. Bid.

[6]

In the Easter holidays we saw the first productions of Shaw's *St Joan* and Flecker's *Hassan*, both hugely enjoyed. Then I went back to Eton to study for the School Certificate examination, which I passed satisfactorily in July, while at Halcot my mother's insomnia grew steadily more persistent. Dr Hinds vainly prescribed remedy after remedy, and she took to her bed for some days. Above all she longed to get rid of Halcot, which now seemed to her more and more of a prison: gilded bondage perhaps, but dreary and unnerving.

I have thought a lot about everything and rather come to the conclusion that perhaps it would be better to stay on here. Daddy wants to, so do you in your heart of hearts, I believe, and it is really rather a lovely home, with the books and all, isn't it? I have told Daddy that I would like him to do what *he* would like best. After all, we could always go to London for a time in the winter. I am not so weak and vacillating as I expect you will think, but being ill and in bed like that made me feel discontented with everything, and I felt I should be happier if I got away from here. But I am sure happiness does not lie in doing that sort of thing.

She was also bothered by the lack of a cook. The agencies told her that 15,000 servants had been engaged for the Empire Exhibition at Wembley, so the shortage was acute. Eventually a possible cook was reported and an interview arranged: 'Deirdre and I went to meet the cook at the Langham Hotel, but she never turned up. Everyone there looked like a cook and we questioned several, but all to no purpose.'

We went together to the Eton match at Winchester, and on the way back she wrote: 'We had seven hours together today, but they seemed to go very quickly. *How* I loved hearing you say the poems, but I did *not* like saying goodbye to you.'

At Halcot she encouraged herself by resigning from the Girl Guides and acquiring a wireless (crystal) set, but her insomnia and depressive lethargy continued. She enjoyed a month's visit from her mother in July and often took her to London for the day. Before she left Lady Agnes wrote in her diary: 'Went to London. Had passport photographs taken. So ugly that Sibbie tore them up.' (More than fifty years later Deirdre did exactly that, and almost missed her holiday as a result.) One day they lunched with Duff at the Carlton Hotel, and my mother

> loved seeing him. I told him you were reading a good deal of Beerbohm, Chesterton, Belloc, Strachey and Whibley, and he said: 'Well, he's in good hands.' He was very nice and said he sleeps like a log and enjoys every minute of his life.

No one could decide what to do about the summer holidays. The Ozannes were off to a cure at Aix-les-Bains, so Hardelot was not considered, and as a last resort a suite of rooms was taken in the Grand Hotel, Eastbourne. The weather was appalling and I went to bed with influenza. We decided to cross the Channel, and a man came to photograph me in bed for my passport.

Rupert at Eastbourne 1924

But the weather at Dieppe was no better, and the few games of golf we played were penitential. One day my father, who was a chain-smoker, was crouching in a bunker, trying to light his next cigarette in a gale, and I heard him mutter: 'Everyone knows that French cigarettes are made of straw, but that's no reason for their matches to be made of asbestos.'

We spent a good deal of time in the Casino, where, as at Etretat, my height persuaded the authorities that I was old enough to gamble, and there we made friends with Lady Blanche Hozier, the mother of Clementine Churchill. Every day she drove from her home to the Casino in an open cab, looking very like Miss Havisham. We all loved her. Many years later, when I went to lunch with the Churchills at 10 Downing Street, Clemmie greeted me with: 'I knew your mother,' to which I answered: 'And I knew yours,' which surprised and pleased her.

[7]

The winter half of 1924 at Eton was the first that I positively enjoyed. Hitherto, in Gibbon's words, 'instead of repining at my long and frequent confinement to the chamber or the couch, I secretly rejoiced in those infirmities, which delivered me from the exercises of the school and the society of my equals. As often as I was tolerably exempt from danger and pain, reading, free desultory reading, was the employment and comfort of my solitary hours.' Now, as a Language Specialist, I found the work interesting, and for the first time I was well enough to play football without dread: I was never any good at it, but it was agreeable to be one of a team instead of alone in the sickroom.

But I still found time for plenty of free desultory reading, discovering Conrad and Meredith, besides many lesser writers: 'I spent Madge's £1 on Chesterton's Life of Dickens, Maurice Baring's *Diminutive Dramas* and a Life of W. S. Gilbert.' I also developed a passionate interest in Acrostics, soon to be superseded by Crosswords: the boys' maid who cleaned my room took a great interest in these and was always asking how I was doing with 'them Cross Questions'.

Meanwhile on 29 September my mother wrote: 'After lunch I took Deirdre to Crayford, where she was duly received into the Church of Rome. She was very sweet and is very pleased about it. So is old Father Carroll.' Then came another Paris holiday with Marie Ozanne. 'On the way to Octave Gréard we stopped to watch the funeral procession of Anatole France. There were *masses* of flowers and *crowds* of people. I simply love Paris.' Duff had decided to leave the Foreign Office and try his hand at politics. At the end of October my parents travelled to Oldham in Lancashire to canvass for him at his first election, in which he came top of the poll.

Jelly Churchill was due to give up his house at the end of the school year, and this November his boys and old boys gave him a huge farewell dinner in the Gymnasium.

Uncle Duff made an excellent speech with some very amusing jokes in it. I think Jelly loved it. We gave him three cheers and sang 'For he's a Jolly Good Fellow'. It went on from 7.30 till 10.15. Uncle Duff stayed the night with Jelly and came to Chapel this morning, after which I walked about and talked to him. Then Diana arrived in a lovely Rolls-Royce with Lord Wimborne and fetched him away. He gave me £1. What do you think of that?

After Long Leave, during which we saw Gerald du Maurier in *The Ware Case* and heard Chesterton lecture on 'What is Wrong?' in Westminster Cathedral Hall (I was fascinated by his huge bulk and his one tiny chin nestling on several larger ones), my mother took Deirdre to another Retreat at Grayshott:

18 Nov.   Yesterday we went to the chapel for the first instruction, and what was my *horror* to see a Dominican priest but *not* Father Bede Jarrett! I could have cried with rage and disappointment. He has got a tiresome, rather typical clergyman's voice and a fat face. His name is Father Swaby or something . . . At the second instruction this morning the priest was a bit better. Deirdre rather likes him.

19 Nov.   We like the priest more and more. The nuns here never go out except when they have to go to the dentist.

21 Nov.   Deirdre and I are sorry the Retreat is nearly over. We have *thoroughly* enjoyed being here and we like Father Swaby very much indeed.

On the same day she wrote to her mother:

You came so vividly before my mind when the priest was speaking about how we should always make excuses for the sins of our neighbours. You have *always* been *wonderful* in that way. Deirdre and I talk in our room, but otherwise there is the Blessed Silence, and the nuns move about so peacefully and quietly. It is a *most* soothing atmosphere, and the food is delicious, all so fresh, clean and carefully prepared. A nun reads aloud during meals.

From the beginning of December my father took 35 Great Cumberland Place for four months: it was a charming house, containing, to my delight, nine hundred carefully catalogued books. My mother's old friendship with Wilfrid Meynell ripened. She visited him several times at his flat in Orchard Street, off Oxford Street, and took me there in the holidays. She also took me to lunch with Katharine Asquith, where we met Hilaire Belloc. He explained to us at some length how easy and cheap it was to build a house, and drew us a sketch to prove his point. He was one of the best and most amusing talkers imaginable.

Wilfrid Meynell introduced my mother to his protégé the Irish Catholic writer Shane Leslie, who took her dancing to the Fifty-Fifty Club. She and I had many discussions about my future, and one day, as we were driving in a taxi through Berkeley Square, she suddenly said: 'I know. You'd better be a man of letters,' and in the end that is, more or less, what I became.

PART SEVEN : OUTGOING IN THY NOON

> She seemed one left behind of a band gone distant
> So far that no tongue could hail:
> Past things retold were to her as things existent,
> Things present but as a tale.
>
> HARDY

[1]

EARLY IN JANUARY 1925 news came of Lady Agnes's last illness. Duff and Sibbie dashed out to Cimiez, outside Nice. In her sleeper on the night-train Sibbie heard her mother calling to her, and sure enough they arrived too late. Duff accepted this death with his usual imperturbability, but to Sibbie it was a disabling blow. Her mother's love, tolerance and good humour had never failed, and now this link with stability was cut. She began to drink more than she could manage, and to talk compulsively to anyone who would listen. A heavy cold was no help, but a week-end at Greatham, the Meynells' family home near Pulborough in Sussex, had a calming effect. She loved and was loved by all the family, including a young girl called Anne Brindley, who was living there and helping to look after Wilfrid.

My cold is much better and the complete rest and peace of this place have made me feel quite well again in what they call myself. I am sure you would love it too. I was never in any place I liked half so well. I went to Mass at Storrington at 8 a.m. and since then have had two delicious meals and read all the time in an exceptionally comfortable chair by the fire. Wilfrid read to me for a little, some poems by his wife (which made me cry) and some by Wilfrid Blunt. I have hardly set eyes on Shane. He strides about the countryside or writes all day. I do feel so peaceful and rested – such a comfort it is. I think you will like *Diana of the Crossways*. It is almost my favourite. Uncle Duff thinks the heroine is like me.

But London brought back all her insomnia and depression. A cloud of nervous, mental and physical distress descended on her, forerunner of the fatal occlusion less than two years later. She found a dear old neurologist and hypnotist called Dr Woods, whom she liked and trusted, and at his suggestion she spent three weeks of February in a rest-cure at his nursing home, 2 Primrose Hill Road, Hampstead. Here she was visited by Wilfrid Meynell and by a new friend Beatrice Guinness. This remarkable woman – outwardly tough but in fact all kindness and generosity – also lived in Great Cumberland Place, with her two daughters by her first husband, Zita and Baby Jungman. Deirdre was now temporarily a day-girl at the Convent of the Holy Child in Cavendish Square.

To bring some amusement into the nursing home I made my daily letters as long and entertaining as possible: one was fourteen pages long, another twenty-two. Much of the fun was at the expense of my now dearly loved Jelly Churchill. Sunday Private was an hour each week which boys spent under their house-master. Originally it had been devoted to some scriptural subject, but by my day almost every other house-master read short stories or poetry aloud, or discussed current affairs, but Jelly stuck firmly to the old tradition:

> This morning we had our usual Sunday boom from Jelly. As we have finished the *Book of Job*, which we have – or rather he has – been studying for the last sixteen years, he is now launching forth into what he calls 'a brief sketch of world history before A.D.' Pretending to take notes, most boys use this time to write their weekly letter home, and one boy (a different one each week) is detailed to ask intelligent questions at appropriate points. Yesterday at lunch I held Jelly in check for a long time talking about the Moroccan question and the Riffs. It was rather comic, as he doesn't really know anything about it, and I don't care if all the Riffs are blown up tomorrow. They're merely Riff-raff! I didn't start this story so as to bring in the joke: it just came naturally. Jelly never stops saying what a marvellous thing inoculation is, and he himself has had a snorting cold for about a month.

My mother was back at Great Cumberland Place in time for my Long Leave, during which I went with Baby Jungman to see John Barrymore's *Hamlet*, the first I had seen and most impressive. Early in March came another ten happy days at Greatham:

> *Me voici établie dans cette maison pleine de calme et de bonheur.* Deirdre is coming. How I wish you were too! I love being here. I read Clare's

Diary [from Meredith's *Richard Feverel*] and 'Marpessa' [by Stephen Phillips] to the company last night – not well. Afterwards Wilfrid read us some poems by various moderns – Ralph Hodgson, Julian Grenfell etc. W.M. tells me such interesting things about all sorts of celebrated people and is so sweet. I love him.

At Eton I was 'deep in *Anna Karenina*', buying a high-necked sweater and the poems of Oscar Wilde. 'This morning I read a few extracts from Carlyle's *Historical Sketches*. I rather like his style, which is said to be so tiresome.' Back came an answer from Greatham:

I always had a passion for Carlyle and loved his style. So should you, as I saturated myself in his writings just before giving you birth. I also attended lectures at King's College on Carlyle and Ruskin, and the lecturer gave such preference to Carlyle that he has set me, rather ignorantly, against Ruskin for life.

When she was back in London this exchange took place:

'Sometimes I wish you took a little interest in religion.'
'Darling, I'm not a complete Heathen, as you seem to think, but it seems to me that everyone should have full time to make up his mind.'
'I am quite *overjoyed* to hear you are not a complete Heathen, and am full of lovely secret hopes. I slipped into Spanish Place on my way home, burnt some candles and said some vague prayers, chiefly about you. I am in rather a Timon of Athens mood today.'

After yet another bout of influenza, during which I read five or six books, I went to the doctor (that same one who might well have killed me in 1921), 'to see if I was fit enough to play squash and other games again. He said I was, but that I mustn't do anything strenuous. I told him he needn't worry about that. I played a little squash this afternoon, but was too limp and lethargic to pursue the ball and merely prodded feebly at it when it came towards me.' I was constantly copying out poems and enclosing them with my letters.

Towards the end of March the cloud descended again:

The less one does, the less one can do! Having done nothing but lie in bed all day I have hardly the energy to put pen to paper. I am *very* depressed and with plenty of reasons. I should like to be beautiful, brilliant, adored by all and especially a small select few, have several talents and no money-worries, abounding health, and to be a nailer at crossword puzzles, besides a few other things. Oh if only we could get rid of Halcot!

To which I could only answer:

> You *are* beautiful *and* brilliant, and you are certainly adored by all and sundry. Your health will soon be as right as rain when I take charge of you. It's no earthly use worrying about Halcot. I do love you so.

The Easter holidays passed serenely at Halcot, and in May Deirdre went for a term to the Holy Child convent at Mayfield in Sussex. It was her first separation from our mother and neither of them enjoyed it. Deirdre, after deciding she would wait three days before running away, bore it stoically, and my mother attended another Retreat at Grayshott, this time with Father Bede Jarrett himself. On the Fourth of June I got leave to go to London and together we saw the dramatisation of Somerset Maugham's story *Rain*. Next day:

> You were so sweet yesterday, and I didn't much like leaving you. Life seems kind of solitary nowadays. I feel I waste my time dreadfully, but don't quite know what to set about doing. I was not made for a hermit's life and don't care at all for solitary confinement.

At Eton I was by now in the Library, the small governing body of the house. The others all became close friends, but the only one I continued to see in later years was David Smith, who eventually became head of the family business W. H. Smith & Son. Now in July 1925 he very kindly asked me to his country home at Greenlands on the Thames for the first day of the Henley Regatta. I felt very shy in the large family party, and my shyness turned to horror when after lunch I was put into a double-sculled boat to row up to the course with David's father Lord Hambleden. He was outwardly stern and rather frightening, and he assumed, quite wrongly, that I knew something of rowing. He took the stroke position, and by keeping my oars almost out of the water and following him carefully I *just* managed to avoid hitting him in the back at the end of each stroke. The distance seemed endless and when we reached the enclosure my best clothes were drenched with sweat.

Undeterred by my incompetence David asked me to stay for part of the summer holidays. I told my mother of this and she answered: 'It's very kind of David to ask you to stay with him. I should miss you very much, but I mustn't be selfish and make you into too much of a recluse.'

To which I answered: 'I have absolutely no intention whatsoever of going to stay with David. Did you really think I was going to leave you, darling?' I did occasionally wonder what was going to happen when I was what is called grown-up, but luckily I have always had the ability to push non-immediate worries out of my mind. Now, as the school year ended I wrote:

> I'm sure I shall enjoy *Hay Fever*. Jelly is still explaining why the Eton VIII were beaten: it is getting a trifle tedious. He has found a scholarship of sorts at Balliol that I might do in December: I think it sounds fairly easy. Poor Jelly, I'm afraid he is getting rather sad about giving up the house.

Our summer holidays began at Cabourg on the Normandy coast, but the weather was atrocious and my only memory is of Frenchmen doing P.T. on the beach in the rain. One day the barber who came to shave my father said he could not understand why we went to the North of France instead of the South, so we immediately took train for Cannes, whence we quickly moved along the coast to Juan-les-Pins. The idea that the South of France was suitable for summer holidays as well as winter ones was only now beginning to be accepted, and when we got to Juan we managed to get rooms in the first of its many hotels, which was almost completed. The sun shone and we enjoyed everything there, including the sight of my old hero E. Phillips Oppenheim floating in the sea like a red-faced porpoise.

On the way home we stopped two days in Paris, visiting Versailles and Malmaison, where I was so interested in the library, and in the contrast between the two houses, that next day on the quays I bought for 140 francs the twenty-six volumes of Thiers's *Histoire du Consulat et de l'Empire*, which greatly impeded our journey home. We also visited the cemetery of Père Lachaise and inspected the graves of Balzac, Chopin, Musset, Sarah Bernhardt and Oscar Wilde. My mother had discovered and read with much enthusiasm the works of the Catholic novelist Léon Bloy. She consulted Shane Leslie, who replied:

> I am delighted that you have finished Léon Bloy's *Le Désespéré*. I regard it as one of the great Catholic novels. I expect his *Âme de Napoléon* is really his masterpiece and the best to translate for the English public. But if you care to do *Le Désespéré* I will revise it and write a scintillating introduction.

Mother and son 1925

She immediately began this translation, but, like all her other literary beginnings, it remained unfinished. Shane accompanied her on another week-end to Greatham, when she outrageously disregarded the rule of her Order. Shane wrote to me many years later:

> If I ever finish my memoirs there must be a few scenes memorably Sybilline – such as her arrival at Victoria Station in full Dominican dress, white as fuller's earth, on her way to Greatham. She would have made a perfect Martha in those days, except that she would have made Our Lord miss his train to the Lakes, after she had arranged to supply scenes for some miraculous fishing, and forgetting Lent would have trudged into the wilderness carrying a picnic basket for Him from Fortnum & Mason. She was as exquisite, dreamy and generous as that – busy thinking little acts of practical phantasy to please (and of course amuse) her friends.

[2]

I began my last year at Eton in a different house and with a new house-master, E. W. Powell. He was a good and nice man but reserved and with little small talk. He was still a hero for having won the Diamond Sculls at Henley and we found him more easy-going if less engaging than Jelly. (He was killed in a climbing accident with three other masters in 1933.) I was now near the top of the school and for the first time came into direct contact with the brilliant and glamorous headmaster Cyril Alington, whose effectively histrionic sermons on Sunday evenings held everyone spellbound. I reported some of his stimulating and window-opening sayings in school:

> Alington started off by saying: 'Do you think Napoleon was a bit of a cad?' I said 'Yes' (the obvious answer). He said 'So do I,' which was quite a good beginning. Then he talked at great length, saying how remarkable it was that Napoleon was not a Frenchman, and that, had he been one, he might not have had all his dreams of world conquest, as the French are so narrow-minded. And that the French had never really understood him, any more than they understood Napoleon III, and wondering what would have happened had Napoleon stopped short in 1802 and spent the last twenty years of his life consolidating his empire and his dynasty.
>
> This afternoon Alington lectured on Jane Austen. He said that men were always supposed to be brave but stupid, and women cowardly but artistic, whereas really exactly the opposite is true.

I also caught a glimpse of the Poet Laureate:

> I went and heard Robert Bridges in School Hall. He is a dear old man with a very attractive appearance – every inch the poet. He read poems of his own, some of which I thought quite good, and a little Milton. I was sitting rather far away from him, and his voice wasn't very strong, but I enjoyed it.

Now came an event that affected the whole course of my life. Peter Fleming, a great swell in the school – Captain of the Oppidans, in Pop and all the rest of it – persuaded the Headmaster to sanction two performances of a modern play in School Hall (hitherto only dim scenes from Shakespeare in the Cloisters had been allowed). He found a perfect director and general manager in Miss Oughterson, the Dame in College, and between them they chose Shaw's *Androcles and the Lion* as their play. In search of actors Peter questioned his friends, and it was probably David Smith who told him that I had been good in some house charades a year ago, so I was engaged to play the part of Ferrovius, the Christian slave. Peter doubled the parts of the lion and Spintho, the coward. John

Lehmann played the Roman captain, Quintin Hogg Megaera, and Ava[1] the menagerie-keeper. I had no idea that my part was meant to be funny, and the admirable Miss Oughterson wisely forbore to tell me, but I so over-played it for straight drama that it must have become funny, though the master who reviewed the play in the *Eton College Chronicle* said, 'Perhaps his serious acting did more than anything else to make the play interesting as well as amusing.' We gave two performances early in December. My mother brought a party of eight, including my father, Deirdre, Beatrice Guinness and her daughters.

> My dearest belovedest boy, I really can't tell you how much I enjoyed the play, or how well I thought you acted. It was altogether splendid and not half enough appreciated by the rather luke-warm audience.

Whatever the temperature of the audiences, we netted £75 for an Eton charity, and I enjoyed every moment of the enterprise. A few days later I travelled to Balliol and failed to win a scholarship, but was deemed to have done sufficiently well to be admitted to the college without further examination.

My mother reported from Halcot: 'No news much. Augustus John and his wife came to lunch. Shane has cut down an oak-tree in the wood. He is bringing his wife and two children here for Christmas. I was transported with pride and joy on reading the *Chronicle*.' Then she retired to bed and dictated to Deirdre this sprightly letter:

> My own darling Church of England son, Beatrice says she likes me better than any of her friends, but I believe it is mere talk. She dragged me to three sales yesterday, which have quite broken my spirit. Dear sweet lovely little Deirdre was left alone the whole afternoon in consequence.
>
> Drat these idle women and their carryings-on. Mrs Taylor keeps sending me corn-cures and imploring me to insure my life with Scottish Widows as it would bring her in £10. I have given her £5, a carpet and innumerable vegetables, and she still says life is a struggle. Amy, Cissy and Mrs Curtis write to me by every post. None of the ladies of London will send Deirdre any more bits for her blasted patchwork. Your most Catholic mother Bid

---

[1] Basil, Earl of Ava, later fourth Marquess of Dufferin and Ava. Killed in Burma 1945.

[3]

In January 1926 Peter Fleming got permission for us to produce
another Shaw play in School Hall. *The Devil's Disciple* was chosen, with
Peter as the hero Dick Dudgeon and myself as Anderson the minister.
Jack Donaldson played General Burgoyne, and Jasper More Mrs
Dudgeon. Miss Oughterson again presided with great efficiency. My
letters describe the background:

3 Feb.   I am making friends with Ava. He is brilliantly clever and
rather amusing.

7 Feb.   I spent all this morning rehearsing.

8 Feb.   I am doing Literature Extra Studies with George Lyttelton,
who is *most* amusing. This morning he was talking about Macaulay –
extremely interesting. I am reading *Ruy Blas*. Do you remember when
Marie tried to make me, and I hid the book?

12 Feb.   This morning I have read the first two acts of Ibsen's *Lady
from the Sea*, which I like enormously – even more than *Hedda Gabler*.
We had a lecture by a missionary who had been in China for twenty
years and looked it. I listened some of the time and then read another
act of *The Lady from the Sea*. Her old lover has come to take her away –
oh, what is going to happen?

15 Feb.   Yesterday evening in Chapel Alington told the story of 'The
Happy Prince'.

21 Feb.   We rehearsed again last night, and this morning I am going
to say 'Love in the Valley' to George Lyttelton. I shall probably falter
a good deal through sheer nervousness. *Later*. Well, I said the poem to
G.L., only failing for a word once or twice, and thereby shall get off
next Thursday's Early School.

Meanwhile my mother was going through an agonising experience.
The doctors, unable to account for her continued despondency and
poor health, decided in desperation that the cause of the trouble must be
her teeth, so on 15 February she went into that same Bulstrode Street
nursing home where I had so nearly died, to have them all removed.
'How would you like to have no teeth? I shall look like the Witch of
Endor and shan't be able to speak.' A fortnight of pain and fever
followed. 'Dr Furber thinks I shall be a different woman. Let's hope so.'
Then her false teeth were inserted: she hated them always but gradually
grew more or less accustomed to them.

At Eton my enjoyment continued:

4 March   Peter Fleming did not go on the Field Day because he had sprained his ankle, so we spent the morning arranging about scenery, dresses etc with Miss Oughterson. She gave us some coffee and cake. This afternoon I played eleven games of squash with P.F. and won by six to five! [So much for his sprained ankle.]

7 March   Had tea at the Red House with Ava and a very nice chap called Jim Lees-Milne. Talked about Shelley, *Hassan*, Shaw and Oscar Wilde.

9 March   Rehearsing yesterday evening and this morning. This afternoon played a little squash with Peter and played some gramophone records with him and Jack Donaldson in Lubbock's Library.

10 March   This afternoon we played a cross-country golf foursome for $1\frac{1}{2}$ hours over plough, marsh, river, and railway arch. I won. We lost seven old balls belonging to various other people.

18 March   Dress rehearsal of *Devil's Disciple* – chaos.

19 March   First performance a great success. I love the feeling of speaking to a room full of people.[1]

1 April   I have had two enormous meals at the Red House today – one with Peter and one with his brother Ian. They are a charming family.

[4]

At the end of the Easter holidays I again fell ill, and went with my mother to Brighton to recuperate. As usual we enjoyed our time in that health-restoring and well-bookshopped town. Nor did the General Strike from 3 to 13 May interfere with our pleasure. Then I went back to Eton, and my mother, accompanied by Deirdre and my father, travelled to Aix-les-Bains for a three-weeks cure, but it did little good and none of them enjoyed their stay:

A fearful old dud of a doctor arrived. I told him my inside was dropping out, that I had a touch of urticaria and wished to lose some weight. He didn't seem very bright but listened intently to my heart beating with and without a stethoscope.

[1] George Lyttelton, reviewing the play in the *Chronicle*, wrote: 'Hart-Davis struggled nobly, but – well, could Forbes-Robertson play Falstaff?'

My inside aches, I mustn't eat any food and am continually being pinched from head to foot by massaging women.

Back at Halcot, after a more enjoyable week in Paris, she wrote:

I lost 6 lbs altogether, two each week – not very much, but it makes a difference. 10 stone 4 now in clothes. In reading some history this morning I learned that Sir W. Raleigh was imprisoned for thirteen years. This makes me feel more patient.

My last weeks at Eton were almost pure pleasure. I read *Under Western Eyes* and *La Princesse Lointaine*, walked, talked and ate with Peter, David Smith, Ava, Jim Lees-Milne and Peter Cazalet, listened to George Lyttelton on Ossian and the *Anti-Jacobin* and to Uncle Duff on the General Strike, drank stout (on doctor's orders) for my lunch but soon grew sick of it.

13 June   Today Peter and I lunched in College Hall as the guests of Jasper More, who is Captain of the School. It was most interesting and amusing. We sat at the Sixth Form table. Before and after lunch about ten of them chanted long Latin graces, and at lunch they passed round an enormous two-handled cup, out of which each person drank in turn (cider). The Provost, Vice-Provost and Headmaster were at the high table. I had never seen it before, and Oppidans don't realise that all the old customs are kept up. I must say most of the Collegers looked heartily bored.

I managed to come seventh in the school (third of the Oppidans) in the final July Examinations and left with sorrow and affection the place where for the greater part of my sojourn I had been miserable and ill.

[5]

Our summer holiday, one of the most successful, was spent in perfect weather at the still delightfully primitive Hôtel Eden Roc on the Cap d'Antibes. We bathed all day from rocks into deep clear water. A little way offshore was an anchored raft, and swimming out to it one day I got into conversation with a slim young man who was sun-bathing there. He told me his name was Raymond Mortimer, and when I told him I was just going up to Balliol he gave me a lot of useful information about the college. We have remained good friends ever since.

At the end of September my mother took Deirdre to the Avenue

Octave Gréard and handed her over to the Ozannes to be 'finished'. The parting distressed both of them, since in all Deirdre's seventeen years they had been together, except for that one term at Mayfield.

Then came my departure for Oxford. Before I caught my train we had tea at the house of Jack and Lily Gilliat in Stanhope Place, where my mother was to stay for a few days. She told me that my promise not to smoke until I was twenty-one (which I had so far kept) had better be remitted, and next day Peter Fleming and I bought ourselves pipes at Fribourg & Treyer in the High at Oxford and became pipe-smokers for life. Three days later I wrote from Balliol:

> It's a comfort having Peter here. He also feels a bit bewildered and wishes he was back at home. The bathroom is within easy bicycling distance. The universtiy seems to be composed of a large number of boys trying desperately hard to be men, and a few old men pretending to be boys.

My rooms in Balliol were dark and cheerless. There was a lavatory on my staircase, but it lacked window or electric light, and Peter refused to enter it, saying he was sure there was a black man in there already. His rooms in Christ Church were much more attractive and we spent most of out time there, playing on his portable wind-up gramophone the latest tunes: 'Bye Bye Blackbird' was our favourite, and fifty years later the sound of it brings back my growing anxiety for my mother. We saw Strindberg's *Spook Sonata* at the Playhouse Theatre, joined the Oxford University Dramatic Society and were allotted small parts in next term's production of *King Lear* by Komisarjevsky. My tutor was useless and I felt unable to work. In Balliol I met again my Stanmore friend Wyndham Ketton-Cremer, and in other colleges I made new friends in Harman Grisewood, Roger Fulford, John Betjeman, John Sparrow, and Osbert Lancaster; at Garsington I met the Morrells, David Cecil and L. P. Hartley; but all the time my thoughts were far away in Primrose Hill Road, where my mother was once again in the care of old Dr Woods.

[6]

Four days after my departure for Oxford she wrote to tell me of what proved to be her last outing:

> I went to the unveiling of the Guards Memorial – a steady two hours' standing by the Admiralty, all impressive enough, if a trifle long. I

thought of Raymond and Bimbo and could have got up 'a good cry', but forbore.

She was planning to attend another retreat at Grayshott, but the black cloud descended too soon. There were, I think, a number of circumstances which combined to induce the total decline into which she now fell: her increasing insomnia; the yearly autumnal depression; dread of her approaching fortieth birthday; hatred of the false teeth that added an extra horror to the advent of middle age; Deirdre's absence in Paris, which heralded total solitude; and above all my departure to Oxford, which seemed to signal my growing up and eventual separation from her. There were no wild excursions, no desperate drinking, as there had been during the crisis of my illness five years ago; only a turning of her face to the wall, a retreat from the complexities of life, and finally from life itself. As Marie Ozanne wrote later, '*Elle ne pouvait pas faire face aux exigences de la vie*'.

Dr Woods decided that she needed complete rest, and that it would be best if no one, not even I, visited her. We both unwillingly acquiesced in this decision, anxious only to get her well. Had I known that my father, the last person she wanted to see, was visiting her daily I should have insisted on going too. As it was, to the great distress of us both we did not see each other between 14 October and 4 December. It is impossible to know whether my presence would have made any difference, but for the next thirty years I had a recurring nightmare that she was still alive, incarcerated somewhere, and I had failed to visit her for years.

I went up to London several times, so as to feel a little nearer to her, and spent most of the time on three visits to the play of *The Constant Nymph*, in which Edna Best charmed and delighted me.

Dr Woods did his best for a month, but my mother's condition steadily deteriorated, so he called in a leading alienist Sir Maurice Craig, who had seen her in 1921. He reported:

an exaggeration of the mental unrest and mental instability that she showed five years ago. She was always hypersensitive, unstable and somewhat undisciplined, and reacted violently when disturbed. This she tells me is the case today. She conversed freely, fully appreciating how abnormal she was at times. She complained of hearing 'voices' which on occasions she felt she must obey, though at other times she is able entirely to disregard them . . . I look forward to her fully recovering.

On his advice she was moved to a nursing home at 8 St Albans Villas, N.W.5, and her case was handed over to the neurologist Risien Russell. He at once tactfully stopped my father's visits and said I could see her as much as I liked. During this separation I had written to her every day and got back pathetic little notes.

1 Nov. I am very comfortable and happy here, with four special nurses to look after me.

7 Nov. Won't it be Heaven when we meet again, me darlin'. Just you and I.

9 Nov. Darlingest, How I long to see you. Do come soon, *do*.

15 Nov. I do hope I shall see you soon. Sometimes I feel quite sick with longing for a sight of your sweet face.

19 Nov. You are a perfect marvel to get a letter to me every day, and oh how I do look forward to them and enjoy them when they come, you *precious* boy. I don't care very much for Strindberg: he always makes me feel depressed. I am not supposed to read very much. Please send me some oranges or apples.

20 Nov. I arrived at this new home safely this morning and simply love it. I have already slept five hours today and feel sure I shall mend very quickly here. I rather miss Woods and my other nurses, but shall soon get over that, I'm sure. Goodnight, dearest heart. I do love you.

After her death her favourite nurse, Patsy Geoghegan, wrote to me:

She made us all love her, and please don't think I was any kinder to her than the others. It was only that I was with her from the beginning and the other nurse didn't have the 'way' of pleasing her; and being R.C., when she prayed and I answered her, she thought the bad dreams didn't come near, so I had first place with her, and loved her so.

When I looked at your writing I thought, how it seemed to be the one writing in the world your mother loved. The countless times she sent me downstairs to see if there was a letter from you, and when I brought her one, how she would slip under the clothes and hold it next her heart to keep the pleasure of opening it as long as she possibly could. I don't think you will ever know how much she loved you.

I went to the grave on St Patrick's Day with a piece of shamrock which she bet me I would forget to send her. I'm sure she smiled in Heaven.

The last of all my mother's letters to me was written on her dreaded fortieth birthday, which she had now quite forgotten.

26 Nov.   Rupert darling, do come. I am almost dead from too much kindness. E. P. Furber is an archangel. I love you. Bid.

Our reunion on 4 December was all tears and laughter. I came up from Oxford several days a week, and when term ended I took a room in the nursing home, so as to see her every day. Her deadly insomnia was now intensified by terrifying dreams, so that she fought against the sleep she so badly needed. The drugs they gave her had varying effects. On some days she was her normal self, loving and laughing; sometimes she failed to recognise me, and once mistook me for some fancied enemy and threw things at me. When I was not with her I sat in my room struggling through H. G. Wells's new three-volume novel *The World of William Clissold*, which is now forever part of that nightmare time.

The worst days of all were those when some drug released her inmost feelings and, unaware of my presence at her side, she poured out all her remorse for errors in the past, her terrors when she slept, her dreads for the future, in a stream of subconsciousness terrible to hear. As Father Bede Jarrett wrote in sympathy, 'To see those whom we love suffer, to be utterly unable to help them in their suffering, to have to stand and watch, is the real agony of love.' Gradually her brain and her nervous system were worn out by all these excitements and she slowly sank into the lethargy from which there was no return.

[7]

Content thee, howso'er, whose days are done;
There lies not any troublous thing before,
Nor sight nor sound to war against thee more,
For whom all winds are quiet as the sun,
All waters as the shore.

SWINBURNE

They brought her to die in a nursing home in Queen Anne Street, only a few hundred yards from the house where she was born. Deirdre came back from Paris, and the three of us took rooms in the Langham Hotel round the corner. She was in a coma now, and there was nothing for us to do but wait. Duff came and wept. We stayed by the bedside helpless.

Towards the end, under the stress of almost unbearable emotion, I experienced, for the only time in my life, the sensation of being momentarily disembodied. From a top corner of the room I seemed to be looking down on my mother in the bed, Deirdre and myself sitting each side, my father standing at the foot. Then I was back in my body again.

At last, on 3 January 1927, the terrible death-rattle faded, and her long struggle was over. When I went in for the last time she was dressed in her white Dominican habit, lovely and serene, watched over by nuns in candlelight. I put into her hands the little book of poems that I had so often recited to her, kissed her marble brow and left her for ever. Later, when I looked down into the deep, deep grave at Kensal Green, I realised that my life, as I had known it so far, was over.

EPILOGUE : THE FADING VISION

As much as in a hundred years she's dead
Yet is today the day on which she died.

D. G. ROSSETTI

IT IS MORE than fifty years since she died, and I have seen her only
fleetingly in dreams, which are hard to hold or recapture: 'our dreams
pursue our dead and do not find'. A further unexpected deprivation was
comfortingly explained long ago by Sir Thomas Browne: 'Another
misery there is in affection; that whom we truly love like our own selves,
we forget their looks, nor can our memory retain the idea of their faces;
and it is no wonder, for they are ourselves, and our affection makes their
looks our own'. Drawings and photographs are reassuring, but memory
alone can conjure up only 'a shadow like an angel, with bright hair'. My
own hair is white now, and hers was still golden when she died: 'I wither
daily: time touches her not'. Gradually through the years I have moved
from her son to her contemporary, and now I am old enough to be her
father. As her friend Alice Meynell wrote:

> Nay, nay! too new to know
>   Time's conjuring is, too great to understand.
> Memory has not died; it leaves me so –
>   Leaning a fading brow on your unfaded hand.

APPENDIX A : MADGE AND WALTER CRUM

MY AUNT Madge Hart-Davis was two years older than Richard and from early youth she was interested in scholarship. While she was studying Egyptology under Wallis Budge at London University she fell in love with an extremely handsome young Scotsman called Walter Ewing Crum. He was eleven years her senior and unhappily married. At Eton and Balliol he had spent most of his time playing the violin: he was a fine performer, but when his teacher told him he would never be a great violinist he abandoned music and turned to Egyptology, especially to Coptic, the language of the early Egyptian Christians: 'our Coptic Apollo', his friends called him.

Madge and Walter Crum

He returned Madge's love, but his wife refused to release him. Luckily he had an ample private income. He and Madge decided to elope to the Continent and devote their lives to compiling a Coptic dictionary. When all arrangements were made, Madge wrote to her mother to confess her plans, and to Walter arranging a rendezvous at Victoria Station, but she made the classic mistake of putting the letters in the wrong envelopes, and there was considerable confusion before they finally made their escape.

They settled down in a flat in Vienna and began work on their dictionary. In January 1914 the Prussian Academy of Sciences in Berlin agreed to publish the finished work at its own expense, but this handsome offer was extinguished by the War, and it was only with great difficulty and the assistance of the American Embassy that they succeeded in getting back to England, leaving all their precious dictionary-slips behind them.

They stayed first in lodgings, then bought a little house at Westbury-on-Trym, near Bristol, and finally moved to an eighteenth-century house on Bathwick Hill, overlooking the whole city of Bath. Madge changed her name to Crum by deed-poll, and this enforced and continuing deception – for Walter's wife never agreed to a divorce – added a secret note of illicit romance to what was anyhow an exceptionally happy and successful alliance. In private Sibbie used to tease Madge, saying 'Where are your *lines*, Crummy?' until she blushed with scandalised delight. Together Madge and Walter worked away, year after year, at the dictionary, until Madge was doing at least half the work, as well as organising the tens of thousands of slips. She was very good at languages, dead and alive, but Walter's gift was phenomenal: no foreign language presented any difficulty to him. Once when Madge said she couldn't read some manuscript written in a minor Greek dialect, Walter said: 'Don't be silly, there's a Portuguese translation.'

The dictionary was eventually published by the Clarendon Press in six parts between 1929 and 1939. Walter was elected a Fellow of the British Academy in 1931, and in 1944 he died. Madge lingered on sadly till 1953. It was always a joy to visit them: Madge so affectionate and cherishing; Walter shy and nervous, but so genuinely interested in everything one was doing as to make conversation with him like talking to a contemporary. Walter's wife survived him, so no mention of Madge could be made, in the dictionary or elsewhere, without betraying her secret or causing an outburst from the legal Mrs Crum. We all loved Madge, and now that they are all dead I am sure she would forgive me for so briefly and inadequately telling her story.

APPENDIX B : MISS JANET CASE
CLASSICAL SCHOLAR AND TEACHER

AN OLD PUPIL [Virginia Woolf] writes:

The death of Janet Case last Thursday will bring back to many of her old pupils the memory of a rare teacher and of a remarkable woman. She was a classical scholar, educated at Girton, and there must still be some Cambridge men who remember her, a noble Athena, breaking down the tradition that only men acted in the Greek play. When she left Cambridge she settled in London and for many years earned her living by teaching, in schools and in private houses, a great variety of pupils, some seriously to pass examinations, others less seriously to read Greek for their own amusement.

Undoubtedly if the pupil were in earnest Janet Case was a highly competent tutor. She was no dilettante; she could edit a Greek play and win praise from the great Verrall himself. But if the pupil were destined to remain an amateur Janet Case accepted the fact without concealing the drawbacks and made the best of it. The grammar was shut and the play opened. Somehow the masterpieces of Greek drama were stormed, without grammar, without accents, but somehow, under her compulsion, so sane and yet so stimulating, out they shone, if inaccessible still supremely desirable. And then the play was shut, and with her generous tolerance for youth and its egotism she would let herself be drawn into argument, made to discuss modern fiction, since she had said that Euripides reminded her of Meredith; made to thrash out the old problem of artist and teacher, since she had said that Aeschylus reminded her of Wordsworth. And so by transitions, rising naturally from the play, last night's party was reached, and the frock that was worn and the talk that was talked at last night's party, until even she could stretch her one hour no farther but must cycle off, with her little bag of text books, to teach another pupil, perhaps in Islington, perhaps in Mayfair.

In a pencilled note written a few days before her death she recalled how Lady D. 'used to come to her lesson like a nymph scarcely dry from her bath in a gauze wrap . . . and used to say "My good woman" in an expostulatory tone when I objected to an adjective not agreeing with its noun or some such trifle'. The words, with their humorous appreciation both of the nymph and of the noun, serve perhaps to explain why it was that she, who was both so sound a scholar and so fine and dignified a presence, never held any of those posts that might have given her an academic position and saved her from the stress of private teaching. She enjoyed too many things – teaching a real scholar, and teaching a real worldling, going in and out of pupils' houses, noting their characters, divining their difficulties – she enjoyed them all too much and music and acting and pictures to concentrate upon one ambition.

The little house at Hampstead where her sister taught children, and friends came, and old pupils brought her new problems to solve, made a happier setting for her buoyant and unfettered spirit than any college. Her Greek was connected with many things. It was connected, naturally, seeing that she was the niece of Sir James Stansfeld, the reformer, with the life, with the politics of her day. She found time for committees, for the suffrage, for the Women's Co-operative Guild, of which her friend Margaret Llewelyn Davies was secretary; for all the causes then advanced and in dispute. In her way she was a pioneer; but her way was one that kept her in the background, a counsellor rather than a champion, listening to the theories of others with a little chuckle of merriment, opening her beautiful veiled eyes with a sudden flash of sympathy and laughter, but for herself she wanted no prominence, no publicity. She was contemplative, reticent, withdrawn.

In the last years, after her health had broken down, she 'retired'; but the word only signified that she had again extended her scope, this time most happily to enjoy with her sister what London had denied her – a country garden, the grass rides and ancient avenues of the New Forest. What have I done, she once asked, standing under a beech tree, to deserve all this? And echo might have answered: 'You have been yourself.' In the Forest she lived very quietly; she gave up teaching. When an old pupil reproached her, for were there no other girls to whom Janet Case could teach Greek without grammar? she said that the country left her no time. There was always something to do – a bird to watch; a flower to plant; her sister to talk to; and the Forest itself – how could one bear to leave it unseen? But that lesson she had learnt, and to sit by her side when she knew that death was near was to be taught once more a last lesson, in gaiety, courage, and love.

[*The Times,* 22 July 1937]

ACKNOWLEDGMENTS

I AM MOST grateful to all those who have generously given me permission to quote from copyright material, and in particular to the Earl of Oxford and Asquith for prose and verse by Raymond Asquith; to Mr Nicolas Barker for a passage by Sir Ernest Barker; to Messrs A. P. Watt & Son for a quotation from John Buchan's *Memory Hold-the-Door*; to the Provincial of the Dominican Order in England for extracts from the letters of Father Bede Jarrett; to Lady Leslie for Sir Shane Leslie's letters; to Mrs Gilbert Russell for a letter from her husband; to Mrs Nona Hill for the poem by Arthur Symons; to Mr Ivan Moffat for letters of Iris Tree; and to Professor Quentin Bell and Mrs Angelica Garnett for Virginia Woolf's tribute to Janet Case.

Nancy Cunard, bless her, wrote her piece especially for my book and made me a present of it. Peace to her shade.

With the illustrations I have been treated with equal generosity, and I owe gratitude to Mr Romilly John for the drawings by Augustus John; to Mr Ivan Moffat for the drawing by Curtis Moffat and for a photograph of the John drawing of Iris Tree; to Mr Ben Nicholson, O.M., for the portrait by Mabel Pryde Nicholson; and to Mrs Liza Banks for the portraits and drawing by William Nicholson.

The Hoppner portrait of Mrs Jordan is in the Iveagh Bequest at Ken Wood, and I give thanks to the Curator and the G.L.C.

The portrait of Lady Fife by Sir Francis Grant belongs to the Duke of Fife and is at present at Kinnaird Castle. Through the kindness and enterprise of Mr Duncan Kennedy of Banff and the generosity of Mrs Barbara Macpherson of Mulben I am able to reproduce this excellent photograph of an engraving of it.

The portrait of Lady Erroll I owe to the kindness of Major R. A. Carnegie.

The Kottler bust of Max Michaelis is in the Michaelis Collection in the Old Town House, Cape Town. My thanks are due to the Curator, Mr J. C. Haak, and to Mr Cecil Michaelis.

The photograph of Father Bede Jarrett was kindly lent me by Father Bede Bailey, O.P., and the one of Walter Crum by Mr and Mrs John Crum.

I have also been helped in many ways by Sir Martyn Beckett, Viscount Chandos, Mr John Gore, Dr Thelma Gutsche, Sir Alan Lascelles, Mr Ernest Mehew, Father Martin Salmon, O.S.B., Mrs Norah Smallwood, the late Susan, Lady Tweedsmuir, and several members of my family. My fervent gratitude to them all.

R. H.-D.

INDEX